nearly
ORTHODOX

*on being a modern woman
in an ancient tradition*

ANGELA DOLL CARLSON

Ancient Faith Publishing

CHESTERTON, INDIANA

Nearly Orthodox

On being a modern woman in an ancient tradition

Published by:
Ancient Faith Publishing
(formerly known as Conciliar Press)
A Division of Ancient Faith Ministries
P.O. Box 748
Chesterton, IN 46304

Printed in the United States of America

ISBN 10: 1-936270-96-X
ISBN 13: 978-1-936270-96-5

"Want & Need" was first published under the title "Have & Want"
in *St. Katherine Review*, Volume 2, Number 2
"Body and Blood" was first published in *St. Katherine Review*, Volume 3,
Numbers 1 & 2

Cover photo: Sean Williams and Thom Wolfe

CONTENTS

INTRODUCTION

Faith is homesickness. . . . Faith is a lump in the throat.
Faith is less a position on than a movement toward, less a
sure thing than a hunch. Faith is waiting.

—Frederick Buechner

There is something to be said for beginning. Beginning has some intention to it, some urgency. We are born into beginning. I began life as a Catholic. I was born into that beginning. It was a part of my identity, as much a part as knowing I was born into an American family, knowing I was born into the Doll family.

There was no separation between this part of my life and any other part. We were German Catholics on the west side of Cincinnati, Ohio. We lived on streets named for the neighborhood house builder's daughters—Loretta, Olivia, Omena—in dull red brick houses that wore wide board trim and had sprawling, sloping yards. Some families in the neighborhood were only a generation or two from the immigrants who had settled this part of the city. We took pride in heritage and history, family and faith. We walked the short, hilly distance to the local parish church that also housed our school and to the local pharmacy, restaurants, and barbershop owned by the families of my classmates. This was comforting for me. I knew who I was in the world.

If beginning has its urgency, its starting point, becoming is progressive and ponderous. It is organic and sometimes slow growing. I began life as a Catholic, but now I am becoming Eastern Orthodox. It feels as though it is taking forever, and perhaps it is taking forever.

This story begins in the middle, the muddy middle. Present tense is the middle of a moment, and in each of these given moments there is some kernel of meaning—sometimes only the size of a dust mote floating from the light fixture above my head, settling into me, adding to the collection of meaning that defines me. This story begins in the middle because I am in the middle, always nearly at my next destination: middle-aged, middle-income, middle-class, the muddy middle.

Chicago, where I live now, is built on a grid. The streets run north and south, east and west. For the most part, it's an easy city to navigate; landmarks are tall buildings or noisy trains with color-coded identifiers. In some places diagonal streets, left over from old Indian trails, cut through the grid—Milwaukee, Elston, Clybourn. The places where three streets intersect are most often congested and convoluted, traffic starting and stopping, everyone facing forward and looking ahead, using mirrors to see where they've been and peripheral vision to change lanes. At these three-way intersections the traffic is a nightmare. It is as though in the middle of these intersections we lose our way.

Those diagonal streets, those moments left from our long-gone past, seem to throw off our sense of direction and make us unsure of where we're going and where we've been. We edge through, inching or lurching, looking in all directions to sense the traffic, the danger, the disruption. This story that begins in the middle, the muddy middle, relies on the intersection of memory, intuition, and intention. These are places where those three streets come together.

The mapmaking of this book, my spiritual geography as it were, depends on those intersections of the past, the present, and the future. They are intricately woven. They are sometimes congested and confusing. This book is divided then into three parts that form a sort of compass to help guide the reader through—East and West, Giants in the Road, and Into the Roar.

The first street at the intersection is my own past, laid out in the section entitled East and West. It is where I have been, what I've discovered, where I've been injured, and where I've found healing. It is the beginning of the story.

The next street that crosses lays out the external struggle. Called Giants in the Road, it details the obstacles to my conversion—my checklist of deal-breakers, my social anxieties, my lack of consistency and propensity to cuss at inopportune moments.

The last street crossed I call Into the Roar. It is that sideways-jutting street, the one that causes the trouble at every intersection it joins. This street is the unknown, the intense, the unseen. While there were giants in the road, obstacles blocking the path, the lions roaring from the tall grass were the mystery, the unknown, and what lies ahead.

One doesn't become Orthodox by simply being baptized or chrismated (which is to accept the blessing of oil on my forehead, my hands, my throat, my feet, signifying acceptance into the Orthodox Church). Becoming Orthodox means that I will be practicing this way of living, this way of thinking, this way of moving and praying until death, and I will probably always fail in one way or another. The road to chrismation has been long so far—spanning several years, three communities, two cities, and a number of long chats with priests to date. Every step is a struggle. It's clear to me as I sit in the traffic at these intersections that this is a story that begins in the middle, the muddy middle, and it finds me moving East from the West; it finds me fighting giants in the road; it finds me moving into the roar.

PART I

EAST AND WEST

East is east and west is west and never the twain shall meet.

—Rudyard Kipling

Where matters of faith are concerned, everything is remedial.

I have become a pilgrim of sorts. I never imagined myself taking this road. Though the destination is not new, the road is new.

I can easily say that meeting God on a regular basis has been a habit I've fostered. The mystery, the wonder, the practice—I'm all about it. In my best moments, I suppose I thought

I had already arrived. I thought I was there, sipping mai tais with God on a white beach somewhere, palm trees waving in the warm tropical wind. In my worst moments, I thought I'd at least be boarding a plane to get there.

That I'm on foot and taking this ancient road comes as a surprise. This road is dusty and wide. It can be lonely. Sometimes I don't see another soul for miles. In the heat of the day, the road of Orthodoxy is arduous and beautiful. In the calm of the night it is expansive; the moon and the stars provide company, promise, and revelation. But where matters of faith are concerned, everything is remedial. The word comes from the Latin *remedialis*, meaning "healing, curing." Everything about faith is this. Everything.

Catechism classes were called Orthodoxy 101 and were held in the fellowship hall of Holy Trinity Orthodox Church in Nashville. There were only a few of us, sitting around the circular banquet tables in stiff plastic folding chairs at 7 PM on Wednesday nights, some holding Bibles, some holding notebooks, all waiting for Father Gregory to fill us in on the next part of our catechesis, learning the doctrine and history of the Orthodox Church. When I began, I joked to Father Gregory that I ought to be able to test out of 101 and go right to the 200-level courses. Having been raised Catholic, I thought I already knew what I needed to know about Orthodoxy. How different could they be, East and West?

We talked about the Lord's Prayer and about the Trinity. We talked of the history, the Councils, the Great Schism, and I nodded. I got this. I got the Creed, I got the catechism, I got the history; I got it. Sign me up.

I would answer the questions. I would engage in the discussions. I began to meet with Father Gregory on my own then, to speed the process a little and get myself into Orthodoxy as quickly as possible. I asked about the possibility of moving ahead with the next step in my agenda, becoming chrismated. Because I was already baptized in the Catholic Church, chrismation was my next step to becoming Orthodox. Chrismation is the sealing of the gift, the ceremony of the anointing with oil and the proclamation of faith. I thought it was all that was required for me to get my membership card into Orthodoxy.

Father Gregory listened, and then he advised me to begin with daily prayer and see where that led. So, grudgingly, I did, and that is when everything came to a crashing halt.

I was trying to pray three times each day. I was reading books, collecting icons, and beginning to wrap my fingers around the calendar of fasting and feasting when the immensity of the daily life of an Orthodox Christian finally stopped me in my tracks. It was fuller, richer, bigger than I'd expected. The East was heavy, clothed in mystery and black cloth, and it was all new to me, all new, as far as the east from the west. I was standing on a long, twisting road I did not know, with unfamiliar terrain and uncertain weather, and for the first time I looked down at my feet and saw the mud and sand caked there. I saw my bare feet alongside those of the other pilgrims—all feet bare, all feet caked in mud and sand.

I realized then that we are all on this ancient road, this unpaved and dirty road. We are all at level one; we are all trying to avoid the rocks, the injury, the oppressive heat of the day, and the cool loneliness of the night. We are all seeking the steady beauty of the One who made us, we are all desperate for His breath on our skin, His lips on ours to ease the crushing weight of the world we feel pressing in on that deep, empty place in our hearts. Where matters of faith are concerned, everything is remedial.

CHAPTER I

GROWING UP CATHOLIC

(on beginnings)

Once a Catholic always a Catholic.

—Angus Wilson

S t. Teresa of Avila was our parish, and we attended Mass there because we were Catholic and because we lived within the geographical boundaries of that church. It was my mother's church growing up. Everyone we knew, everyone we saw day to day went to St. Teresa of Avila. We came in the side door, usually a few minutes late, looking for space to fit our family of six. I liked when we sat close to the altar because I wanted to see what was happening.

There were two benches in the narthex of St. Teresa of

Avila. They were situated next to the doors to the sanctuary and faced two great windows into the church. There was no sound system in those days, though the sound of the grand pipe organ could be heard through the heavy oak doors, through the wide plate glass window. When children cried without consolation, their voices would echo in the space in the sanctuary. No one would turn to watch them being carried to the narthex; most parents had been there before. There was no judgment, only recognition of the reality of parenting, the reality of being a child in a setting where they were expected to sit quietly, an unnatural act for children. Quiet is a cultivated skill.

Though I was an introvert, quiet was still something that needed tending, shaping, and forming. Left to my own devices, I'd have stayed home playing alone under my bed or in my closet, the two places in my house that were dark and quiet. Once at the Mass, though, I could be lost in the sounds of the choir and organ and the shafts of sunlight streaming in. I could be lost in the responsorial psalm, the epistle, the incense, the bells chiming when the wine was blessed and the bread broken, becoming more than bread, more than wine, becoming the Body and Blood of Christ Himself, given up for me. I would say the priest's words along with him, having heard them all my life. I would watch the dance of the altar servers; I would wait for the cues for the shifting of the service, the Liturgy of the Word melding into the Liturgy of the Eucharist. My brothers would follow along in the missal, pointing out page numbers to count how much longer they would be required to sit quietly; but I was content in that moment, right then.

The Mass held its own kind of quiet, its own brand of peace, and I welcomed it once I was there. At home we were always playing catch-up, running headlong into the chaos, and filling potholes with whatever we had in our pockets. The Mass took everything in stride—crying babies, dropped missals, latecomers. The Mass knew its form and its purpose. We came to be a part of something that had been established, tried and true. We were there to practice. We learn like this, being there, practicing. Sometimes it is the only way we do learn to wait, learn to be quiet, learn to value those moments of peace and quiet. Sometimes it is the only chance we have to enter in, the only opportunity to be emptied, to be filled, to be ready. Practicing the quiet at the Mass kept me fueled for whatever happened during the week at home or at school.

THE FIRST TIME I RODE A TWO-WHEELED bike, it was with my older brother J.D. standing behind me, both hands on the back of the wide leather seat, his legs straddling the back wheel to keep it steady. I was nervous. I did not want to fall, but more than that I did not want to fail. J.D. spoke quick directions into my ear, using phrases like "it's easy," "don't worry," "keep pedaling," and "just go with it." It was his new Schwinn—racing red and shiny chrome—and my dirty white sneakers barely met the thick black pedals. My brother instructed me to straighten my legs to put pressure on the top pedal, to push off and get the bike started. So I pressed into it and pedaled while he held the seat and ran behind me guiding the bike, keeping it steady as he held both hands on the wide leather seat.

I was beginning to get the hang of it, feeling the balance of the bike, my pedaling working against the pull of gravity with each pump, each straightened leg, each bent knee. I turned to tell him I could do it on my own, and when I turned to tell him he could let go, I saw him standing a block down, waving and smiling. Then I hit the telephone pole.

J.D. came running up to me and, ignoring the bike, he helped me to my feet, checking the damage to my head and limbs as I apologized over and over. It was his brand new bike. I was afraid of breaking something he valued so much. I did not want to disappoint him.

My older brother and I are only seventeen months apart. There are photos of us growing up in which he is wearing a certain striped T-shirt one year, and then I am wearing the same shirt the following year. We often sat together in the beat-up recliner in our living room, arms around each other, talking about the neighbor kids or the new baby in our house. We had a lot in common when we were young. We played the same games—Twister, Sorry, and Uncle Wiggly. We watched the same shows—*Gilligan's Island* after school, *Star Trek* on the weeknights, and *Wonderama* on Sunday mornings before church. We liked the same foods—hot dogs and boxed mac & cheese.

At our beginnings we all seem to have a lot in common. And then we grow and change, and suddenly his shirts won't fit my body type any longer, his soldiers don't want to hang out with my baby dolls, his politics don't mesh with my politics. We are still family, but we are not the same. We share a history, a starting point, a beginning; but our becoming shows where the path divides, long after we sat together in the easy chair, long after our parents' divorce, long after I crashed his bike into that telephone pole.

FATHER GREGORY DID NOT LOOK AT ALL like the Eastern Orthodox priests I had envisioned. He was young, at least ten years younger than I. I had to resist the urge to ask the year he graduated high school, to check his ID, to ask for his credentials. His trim modern goatee was a far cry from the long, wiry beards I'd seen worn by the Russian and Greek clergy on the internet, in the movies, on the backs of the many books I'd read on the ancient tradition.

When we met the first time and he gave me the tour of Holy Trinity, I had expected to feel at home there. I looked for the common threads between my own beginnings and this new place. I looked for the lines that intersected here—for the shared history, the shared starting points from before the path divided—East and West.

The feel of the church was familiar, but the faces around me were foreign, the colorful statues of my childhood parish replaced with icons—brooding, ash and gold. The altar was hidden behind a stand of saints, the entry barred by angels, doors, drawn curtains, candles burning, incense-soaked oak pews.

Fr. Gregory spoke in a low voice as he explained the parts of the church, demonstrated the sign of the cross, and venerated the icons nearest the door. When the sunlight hit the high windows of the large room, the shafts of light came to rest on the stone floors. I had never set foot in an Orthodox church before this. I expected the Eastern Orthodox Church to be like the Catholic Church on steroids. I thought I would have some advantage, having been raised Catholic, or at least I would have some crossover; but it was as different from my Catholic roots as my older brother was from me. We were related, certainly, there was the family resemblance, but no one would confuse me for him.

THE ONLY WAY MY MOTHER WOULD AGREE to my moving to Chicago with my band, instead of returning to Wright State University in my third year, was that I'd transfer to Columbia College and finish my degree there. She didn't care what I studied or what else I did with my time, but she expected I would come through the experience with a degree at the very least. It wasn't that she was unsupportive of my musical career, but more that she remembered what it felt like to be twenty years old and a college dropout.

She admits entering college with a goal of achieving her MRS. Certificate, and she achieved that goal by marrying my dad when they met at the University of Dayton. While my mother's continuing education was to have four children in eight years, my dad spent his twenties fighting in Vietnam. He came away with a bronze star and a bad case of post-traumatic stress disorder.

We didn't know about the PTSD when I was growing up; it was the quiet hitchhiker in his duffel bag. It lived in the bottom drawer of his dresser in a brown box where he kept all the reminders of his time in the army. My brother and I used to look through that drawer when no one was around. I didn't understand why it was hidden away. I didn't know what a bronze star meant or what my dad had actually seen and done in the battle zone. We knew we weren't supposed to look at his things, but we did it anyway. Perhaps we knew there was something unseen in that brown box, something that took up space in between the letters and the photographs, the captain's bars and the bronze star. Whatever it was, the space it filled belonged to us, we knew that somehow, and so we stole away time to look through that box in the bottom drawer, putting our fingers on as many of the missing pieces of our dad's life as we could; but my dad was never in that brown box.

Columbia College in Chicago had a program for transfer students in which one could write a program of study, and so I transferred and wrote my own major. For someone like me, who resisted being put in boxes, it was the perfect program. I took acoustics and filmmaking and poetry classes. I took every writing course I could talk my way into. It was a sweet mishmash of words and images and sound and fury. It was the big city accessible to me by the network of trains and buses. I was far from home, writing lyrics and singing for my techno glam punk alternative band, Vertigo in Children. We thought we were edgy. Chicago wrapped its arms around my waist; it bought me coffee and cigarettes. I worked at a record store. I still prayed. All the time.

I only felt lonely when I attended Mass.

Going to Mass was something I did at home with my mom, because it made her happy. Going to Mass was like eating the food Grandma made even if I was not hungry or no longer ate red meat, but I did it anyway without complaint because she went to the trouble of making it, because it made Grandma feel useful and valued. Going to Mass was like sleeping in my old room, seeing the peeling wallpaper I remembered staring into when I was awake at night as a child with insomnia, worry, and fear. Going to Mass was like being surrounded by the kids I knew from school, the neighbors I'd had for years, the old folks who took the collection and acted as usher, all still living there on the west side of Cincinnati, Ohio, all buying houses in the parish and the surrounding parishes. "You're up in Chicago now? I could never do that. Too big and noisy, too dirty." I'd nod and smile, because if I spoke I was afraid I might say something rude.

I only felt lonely when I attended Mass, because though St. Mary's Catholic Church in Chicago was in most ways identical to my own church growing up, it was empty of the people I knew there. It was a safe house at home, but in Chicago it was just another church, another homily, another Eucharist, another organ-fueled droning hymn. I had no business there, I had no pleasure there, and so I stopped going and I forgot about being lonely.

I still prayed, all the time. No matter how I lost track of my dad, my brother, my hometown, the Mass, or my sense of self, I still prayed all the time, whispering words while driving or reading or riding the train. God was the ever-present, the mystical, the immortal, and I imagined myself in constant dialogue with the Divine. An atheist friend at that time referred to God as my imaginary friend, and I didn't correct him. For me God wasn't a topic for discussion. God was not an intellectual endeavor, a theory to be debated, and so I didn't talk about God or Jesus or growing up Catholic, and yet I still prayed, all the time. There was no more reliable a listener. There was no more reliable a presence.

My dad was never in the bottom of that brown box in his dresser. I thought of God as my dad when my dad was absent, which was always. Perhaps it was that I was always looking for him in the wrong places, in boyfriends and punk rock and cigarettes and marijuana. All of these things filled the empty spaces for a while, the spaces that I kept like a prayer on the altar.

So I still prayed, all the time.

CHAPTER 2

JUST ADD WATER

(on baptism)

Water is very forgiving. Everything lifts in water.
—Sarah McLachlan

When I was under the water I could hear voices. Western Hills High School had a pool, and swim lessons were free. I was six years old, waiting in the water in the back of the group, and I was bouncing. The feeling of floating was calm, and the noise from the instructor talking was buffeted by the walls and returned by the rounded ceiling of the room. Everything was echoes. It was like church, and I was bouncing: toes to the floor of the pool, shoulders breaking free, toes to the floor, ears in the water, toes absent floor, head absent surface. I was under the water, and I could hear the instructor's voice droning on, muffled now.

I'm underwater, I thought to myself, feeling proud of my accomplishment. I felt satisfied that even though I'd bounced myself into the deep water, I knew to hold my breath. I was there a moment, calm, floating, closing my eyes, listening in, and then I heard my mother's voice. I heard her screaming, and I opened my eyes. I looked up to see her rushing to the edge and pointing at me. I heard her clearly, "Somebody GET HER!"

I panicked, moving then to try to break the surface and finding I could not. Hands were on me now, pulling me up till my face felt the air again. I took a breath and I was afraid. I had not been afraid when I was under the water, floating there serene and in control. I thought I knew what I was doing under the water. I was dreaming under the water.

They brought me back to the shallow end of the pool and sat me on the cold, concrete edge. I was quiet and I was shaken. I've done something wrong, I thought. I was sure I'd frightened my mother, but I was more afraid I'd disappointed her.

Now, as an adult, I'm uncomfortable in the water. I won't allow my head to go under the water if it can be avoided. I never regained the comfort I felt before I knew to be afraid. When faced with swimming, I admire the water from the shore, from the edge, from the land. I lean into it at the shallow end and I think about that day when I was six years old and I found myself under the water. I think about that every single time.

MY FAVORITE PART OF THE CATHOLIC MASS when I was young was the Liturgy of the Eucharist. The altar boys would bring a basin, a towel, and a small flask of water to the priest. They would pour the water with some gentleness over his hands, his fingers. The priest would speak words I could not hear and then dry his hands on the towel before beginning the breaking of the bread, the pouring of the wine.

For my brothers it meant that Mass was nearly over. Once we reached communion, the number of pages left in the daily missal was manageable. But this moment was holy for me. When this happened in the Mass, I knew we had shifted away from words and into movements. Communion was my favorite part of the Mass.

When I was a kid, we added water to just about everything. We added water to milk, spaghetti sauce, chip dip, juice, and soup. Looking back on it, I realize how little we had in the way of money. Things were always tight for us financially. All we could do to stretch out the grocery bucks was to add water to anything we had. Everything seemed to depend on water. Adding water kept us all afloat.

Under a canopy of trees, less a grove or forest, more an outcropping of overgrowth in the corner of our back yard, I celebrated the Mass. Greeting my friends as they entered my chapel of branches, I'd place white bread and grape juice on the makeshift altar of rocks and mud. From a tiny glass pitcher I'd pour water onto my fingers, then dry them on a small hand towel. Now sanctified, barely breathing, alternately lifting hands, speaking words, making signs of the cross in the air, I celebrated the Mass. I was more than eight and less than ten. I was a weird kid, but my friends were all Catholic and they all came. They thought nothing of it. No one worried we were heretics, no one made jokes. Under that canopy of young trees, that outcropping of overgrowth, I celebrated the Mass.

I might have been an altar server, but the timing was always off. Altar servers were still altar "boys" when I was in grade school. I wanted to be a server so badly. I petitioned, I questioned, I watched, and I listened. I wanted to ring the bells, I wanted to hold the censer, I wanted to be the right hand gal to Father Boyle on Wednesdays at 10 AM, pouring the water on his thick, ruddy hands while the whole school watched. There were secrets for servers, and I wanted to know them.

But girls were not let into the secret club until 1983, when I was 16. By then I didn't care to know those secrets any longer. By then I was discovering new secret things about staying out late and listening to music my parents hated, about drinking cheap watery beer and smoking menthol cigarettes. By then I was looking for the holy moments in myself and noticing less about where I had been. I was looking forward to the future; I was a mess of conflict and rebellion wrapped in an introvert's skin.

METANOIA WAS THE TURNING AWAY AND turning toward. I liked being "emergent" and "missional" in the little church plant we'd begun after Dave and I got married. We wanted to change the world. We wanted to reach into the past and find the ancient Church. We wanted to restart that ancient vehicle, tinker with its engine, add a fuel converter, shine it up and make it attractive to our generation. We wanted the church to be art and music and poetry. We thought we could create that, and we thought we could make it relevant.

We called our church startup Metanoia, based on the Greek work meaning "to change one's mind." We understood spiritual growth as being an outworking of repentance, turning away from sin as we turn toward God. It was a good theory, and we thought it was revolutionary. It certainly was revolutionary for the twenty or so young people who showed up each week, Dave and myself included.

Metanoia was therapeutic; it was restorative, and I needed the repair. I felt homeless in those years before we began the church, before I began to turn away from old habits and my long wandering, and before I knew how to turn toward finding God in church again. It was as if I did not know where to find Him since leaving the Catholic Church. I was unsure whether the presence I felt in quiet moments was real or merely nostalgia.

As a child I knew the embrace of God in the night, cradling me as I fell asleep. I felt those arms. I felt that presence. As an adult I shrugged off those arms time after time, like a teenager squirming from a parent's embrace. I know now, as the parent of teenagers, how desperate the parent is to connect, but words fail and sometimes, too, embraces fail. There grows this wide chasm between us in that middle time, those teenage years, the turning away, the turning towards. The parent stands on the east bank and the child on the west, staring at one another with only water running between us. We are waiting for rescue or redemption or courage to finally make the decision to turn away and walk toward the mountains, the city, the highway, anywhere but the river below.

I wanted to be baptized again at Metanoia. I thought maybe if I could be baptized again, I'd find my fear of water draining away. I hoped being baptized again would give me new insights, new habits, new motivation. I asked my friend and pastor if I could be baptized even though I had been baptized as an infant, but he rejected the idea. In his estimation, my infant baptism had conveyed everything I was seeking. I was baptized once, and it took. Perhaps I already knew this. Somehow I knew that all I hoped for was already in me, somewhere deep, under the water. It only needed to be lifted to the surface. Holy, holy, holy . . .

THE METAL CONTAINER OF HOLY WATER SAT in the corner near the side exit of the narthex of the Orthodox church. The first time they visited the church, my boys spotted it right away, but when they asked me, I did not know how to explain it. There was a cup on top—ornate, pristine, gold. They asked the priest about the holy water, and they asked about the infant baptismal in the opposite corner; they were drawn to the water. He told them it was special, it was blessed water. They were allowed to taste the water when they came, and it was meant to satisfy a deeper thirst. To drink that water meant more than a regular drink of water.

Every time I entered the Orthodox church, it felt as though there was something new I did not know or had not noticed, something more to learn and to practice. For a church so ancient and set in its ways, there always seemed to be a current, a river running beneath it feeding and changing the landscape, so that each time I entered it was both familiar and new.

My grandmother kept holy water in a small glass bottle in her home. I imagined she would sprinkle it at the doorways for protection or blessing, but I never knew her to drink it. I never knew anyone to drink it. The practice coming into church growing up was to stop at the font of holy water on the way in, making the sign of the cross, as a reminder of baptism, confirmation of our commitment and attendance. In this way, the two things were always somewhat connected, the water and the sign. There was some delicacy to the entry process, taking just enough water to wet the fingertips, to feel the water on the skin of the forehead, yet not enough to leave soggy evidence at the chest or to soak into the shirt at the shoulders. Children would reach into the font, spilling on the way out, flicking the water everywhere, destroying what some might have considered the first of the holy moments of Mass; but the church was made for the diversity of the family, and grace was poured out like water from a tap.

On certain days of the liturgical year, the priest would take what looked to be a great silver wand and a bucket filled with holy water. He would process around the church, sprinkling holy water on the congregation, on the Stations of the Cross, on the statuary. I would feel the water on my face and in my hair and think it was magical, hoping that this would finally change things in my life, that it might change me into the person I hoped to be, that it would seep into my skin through my scalp and find in me some magic hidden there, waiting to be lifted to the surface.

When I was growing up Catholic, we would make the sign of the cross as we entered the church, after receiving communion and during the Creed. In our Catholic circles, outside of dinnertime prayers, only grandmothers would make the sign of the cross apart from Mass. They'd make the sign in times of trouble or thanksgiving in lieu of hand-wringing. It looked old school. It felt superstitious. It was a natural act to them, but to me it only worked in context.

In the Orthodox tradition, the sign of the cross is made at various times by various people, bound by tradition on the process—using the right hand, first two fingertips together with the thumb to indicate the Trinity, pinky and ring finger folded into the palm to indicate the two natures of Christ, divine and human. The hand making the movement, forehead to heart, then right shoulder pushing to the left, as opposed to the Catholic practice of left shoulder to right. The mechanism is similar, symbolic but precise in motion; but in the Orthodox tradition it seems to be bound by only a few loose rules on the when—for remembrance, upon mention of the Trinity or the Theotokos or the faithful departed, in times of trouble, in times of joy. It made it hard for me to know how to integrate the action into my own awkward engagement of Liturgy.

So I practiced making the sign at home and in my car in private, to get the pushing instead of pulling action down. I practiced at Liturgy and Vespers less often, waiting and watching until I realized there were no hard-and-fast rules—which almost made it worse, knowing there was no one "right way." I practiced it so often that sometimes when I least expected it, I found I was making the sign of the cross—in the grocery store, in the car, in the middle of the night when I could not sleep. Even a minute later I'd find my fingertips still pressed together— thumb, index, middle—as if releasing the hand position would break the sacredness of that act.

The more I practice these things, the more they begin to mean something deeper to me than they did when I was a child. The sign of the cross becomes familiar, an act now fluid and integrated—like water, on my hands and on my face. When anxiety grips me, making the sign seems to squeeze the fear from my skin, from my forehead and heart, and I find myself back there on the edge of the pool afraid to enter in—so I cross myself. I consider it an admission of the moment, the anxiety, the surrender that comes before jumping into the pool.

I make the sign of the cross in the car and in the kitchen, entering into the practice, getting it right, moving slowly, one toe in the water. At Vespers and Liturgy I may be reluctant still to enter in, reluctant to jump into that water, afraid of doing it at the wrong moment, of bouncing into the deep water of ritual too fast. At Vespers and Liturgy I take my time, and I watch the other people swim along in the current of the motion. I watch from the shore, envious and afraid all at once.

CHAPTER 3

ANGIE IS A PUNK ROCKER

(on schisms and rebellion)

Punk has always been about doing things your own way.
What it represents for me is ultimate freedom and a sense
of individuality.

—Billie Joe Armstrong

I n 1977 I was nine years old. My best friend Margaret had a combination record player and radio in the room she shared with her teenage sister, Mary Jo. We listened to whatever came through the small speaker from our local station, and when that failed, we'd pick through Mary Jo's records and listen to those. Sometimes Mary Jo would dance in while we sat on the floor staring at the cardboard album covers, and she would sing along. She'd smile, take our hands, and pull us up from the floor to dance with her, our awkward preteen moves making her coolness most evident.

No matter how I tried, I could never sing along with Billy Joel's "Only the Good Die Young." I knew all the words and would stay standing for the dancing, but I could never sing along, because I wanted to be good and I did not want to die young. I puzzled over the song for hours, I bought the single for my own small record player at home, but I would stop short of singing along. In my nine-year-old brain I had connected words and intentions and deeds and beliefs and superstitions. I believed that what I spoke or thought had an effect on the condition of my soul. I wanted to be good, and I did not want to die young. Words mattered, and so I never sang along.

My mother's light blue photo album has a crushed spiral binding; the adhesive on the pages has aged to show yellow gummy lines around the curled-up edges of the pictures on each page. Some of those photos show me at the start of freshman year at Seton High School. My Farrah Fawcett hairstyle was in full force on that first day. My mother's faux-leather clutch purse tucked under my arm, I am smiling and apprehensive. Little fish, big pond.

All girls and Catholic, Seton High School is my mother's alma mater, my grandmother's alma mater. This is the family tradition my parents would make sacrifices to uphold. They would scrape together whatever they could; I would work over each summer to help out. We would pay the tuition in dribs and drabs throughout the year. Each time we had accumulated enough cash, I would bring it in an envelope along with my passbook to the school office and wait while the secretary counted it out and typed the numbers into the book, tabbing between the previous balance, the payment, the new balance. The slow descent of the numbers was an accomplishment.

It was important to my parents that I graduate from Seton. The threat was always that they'd send me to the public high school if I did not do my part to keep my grades up and behave well. And I did that, because I wanted to do well, I wanted to behave well, I wanted to be liked.

My parents' marriage was finally beginning to show the wear and tear of their time together, time marred by my dad's service in Vietnam, back before anyone ever talked of post-traumatic stress disorder. I was starting to understand myself as more than a child and less than a grownup, and my parents were pulling apart at the seams. I took both sides, doing my level best to hold us all together, arms stretched out like the figure of Christ on the cross.

I would stare at that giant crucifix hanging above the altar every Sunday morning. Mass was well rehearsed. It was familiar. The Mass was the only unchanging thing in my life, and so I went. It was all I knew.

By the end of my freshman year, I felt myself cast in the pigeonhole I'd been avoiding for so long. Introverted, intelligent, and socially awkward, I was not smart enough to be a brain. I was not tough enough to be a thug. I was not strong enough to simply let myself unfold in my own time.

In high school, apart from our gender, the only other trait we all shared was being Catholic, and it meant next to nothing those first two years of high school. We shared no apparent bond because of our faith. Being Catholic at Seton was redundant in those days. It was the same as saying we were all Cincinnatians or all girls. This is who we were already, when we arrived, when we were born, and it meant nothing in the hand-to-hand combat of social networks. It did not make us equal. It did not make us traveling companions. We were family in name only; we took the connection for granted, and that was a loss.

It's easy to be short-sighted when we're young. We make fist grabs for whatever looks good on the plates before us. By the end of my sophomore year, no closer to knowing what kind of truth I carried around, no closer to peace or wisdom or clarity, I found I was angry. I was angry and afraid. I saw the plates placed on the table; it was the early eighties—big hair, loud colors, pop music—and it was all lacking.

The first day of my junior year at Seton High School, I wore a long black wool army overcoat with heavy black combat boots to complete my Catholic school uniform. The overcoat was a rare find from the St. Vincent DePaul thrift store. It was too warm for the coat, and I could smell the remainders of years of mothball storage and unfiltered cigarettes each time I moved the sleeves near my face. I doodled anarchy symbols on my notebooks though I did not really understand what they meant. I sang lines from hard-core punk rock songs under my breath in the hallways. I sneered and grimaced a lot.

Over the summer I'd given up nondescript for notable. There was something compelling about rebellion, something necessary about avoiding the commonplace, avoiding conformity, especially in a Catholic high school where conformity was the rule. Things were turbulent and uncertain at home. I could not afford a rebellion there because I did not know what held us all together just then. I could not risk at home, but at my all-girls' Catholic high school it was safe. We were held together by the school handbook, by the Sisters of Mercy, by the rule of conformity. Rebellion will leak out any way it can, as a persistent water drip wears away rocks, hillsides, and mountains. Water always finds its way.

I'd been introduced to punk music at a party one weekend at a friend's house. We listened to early works of Bowie and The Clash, and the wheels in my head were greased. We listened to the *War* record from U2, and something stirred in me. We listened to Black Flag and Fear and the Sex Pistols, and all the machinery was running.

Punk rock was more than sweaty singers with sloppy hair and ripped black clothing. It was anguish and it was beauty. It was rebellion and it was redemption. Everything I wanted to say but could not find the words to say was already written there, waiting for me to enter in, waiting for me to join my voice to other voices for which the status quo was sorely lacking. All the anger and all the teen angst and outrage were given an outlet, like Godzilla coming to shore. It felt powerful and productive, and we reveled in that, knowing that when we left the house that night we'd go back to our small lives, far away from the punk clubs and the slam dancing and the outrage and angst.

BE HERE NOW.

The laundry list in my head never stops. It runs on a constant loop, in the car, in the movie theater, in church. It's at its worst when things are quiet, which is why I think the megachurch we attended in Nashville was such a good distraction for a while when we moved there. It was rarely quiet in the megachurch. The entertainment never stopped. The service was precisely designed for my ever-shortening attention span, but it was never enough. I kept looking through the store shelves, tossing out each item, looking for something more, something better, something else. Left to my own silence, I found the entertainment lacking, I found myself lacking, and I would want to move on again, taking the injection of hope that there was indeed something else, the needle penetrating my poor puckered thigh time after time.

It kept me going for a long time, until at last I saw the real emptiness and recognized the reality. It's never enough. I'll always be, on some level, empty and wanting to be filled, and there will never be enough affirmation or entertainment to make me whole. So I run the laundry list of what I have to do and whom I have to call and what I have to remember, and I forget that I need to be here now. I forget that what I have before me is this present moment—food for the journey that I don't realize has already begun in me. I kid myself thinking that the trip is tomorrow, the road is over the hill or next door in the megachurch, in the mall, in the bestselling book I keep hearing about but never buy, or buy and never read.

When I first began attending an Orthodox liturgy, I listened more than I participated. Twice during Liturgy, I would recognize pieces, during the Creed and then later the Lord's Prayer. The Lord's Prayer I could say without reading along in the prayer book, but I would stumble over the words in the Creed every time. There were places that differed, places that jutted to the right or the left, edges that had been rubbed down in other versions of the prayer.

It was the *filioque* that stumped me. The filioque was a chisel in the rock of the church in the eleventh century of Christianity. The words of the Creed were massaged and managed. Words that were whispered into being were then shouted over, pushed and pulled until no more working could be done. The simple words "and the Son" were added to the Nicene Creed, breaking the equal partnership of the Trinity. The Church's issue in 1014 was probably more political than theological and spoke to bigger power issues, deeper rifts, human failings rather than divine intervention, but it persisted. Then in 1054, the Catholics went west, tucking the filioque under their arms, and the Orthodox proceeded east, the words remaining as they had been for a thousand years already.

My priest when I was growing up did not speak much of

the Great Schism. We knew there was one, and we knew it happened in 1054 and that it had something to do with the election of a Pope; but whatever else we were taught left my brain right after I turned in the blue booklets and number two pencils in Father Boyle's classes. While I sat in Orthodoxy 101, the discussion of the Great Schism rang small bells in the back of my head, but the words and the dates were just remnant pencil marks that had been long erased on the ragged pages. I listened to Fr. Gregory talk of the Great Schism, hearing probably for the first time the East's side of the story. It was the words and the politics and the passing of time, the East relying on the growing tradition while the West pressed its face against the glass of reason to look into the future.

The laundry list of what I have to do and what I have done and what I still don't know runs on its loop, and the words float out from the choir and the congregation during Liturgy—Lord have mercy, Lord have mercy, Lord have mercy. From the altar the voice of the priest rings out from behind the "beautiful gate," the holy doors in the iconostasis, which separates the sanctuary from the nave. His voice rings out when the doors are open, when the doors are closed. The sound drifts as though it is the incense-laden air, blown into my face and hair. As the choir leader turns to face us and the Creed begins, I clutch at my prayer book to follow along, because I fall down on the filioque every single time, old habits dying hard and all. But at the end, I close my eyes and feel something rising in me—we look for the resurrection of the dead—because I am resurrected,

because this Creed and these words are lifeblood and witness—
and the life of the world to come. And I am there again, hearing
as if for the first time the words, finding home in those words, in
those lyrics, in those notes lingering on the trail of incense and
memory and redemption and beauty. Words matter.

CHAPTER 4

WRESTLING

(on sitting in discomfort)

*If our lives are made up of a string of a thousand
moments, at some of those moments we look a lot more
spiritually evolved than at others.*

—Anne Lamott

On a high shelf, set apart slightly from the other artifacts strewn around Charlie's house, I spotted the
small, well-dressed statue. I recognized him immediately, one hand holding a globe, the other hand raised in a gesture I see offered by the priest each week at Liturgy now: two
fingers extended, the other digits joined at the tips. It is a gesture
of blessing, the two fingers pointing upward signifying the two

natures of Christ, and the fingers folded into the palm signifying the Trinity.

I pointed to the high shelf. "You have the Infant of Prague here." He looked up absently and then was distracted by a question from behind him before he had the chance to answer. I was surprised to see the statue; it was the only remotely Catholic piece in the house. I knew Charlie to be a hard-core agnostic, but he was also appreciative of beauty and history, of tradition and culture, whether he embraced the intention behind the pieces or not. He spotted the deeper value of the works. He gave places of respect to all the statues—Buddha, Ganesh, Infant of Prague.

He was one of the first people to ask me point blank when I spoke about becoming Orthodox, "Why would you want to do that?" I found that in the moment, I had no answer to that question. The journey so far had been long, and the struggle was constant. I kept thinking at any moment I'd find the road smoothing out, rest areas with fine dining and clean restrooms and maybe a decent cup of coffee to take along in the car, but I was still on foot. The road was still hard and rocky, and I was bleeding all over the angry asphalt and drinking water from puddles in the cracked cement. When Charlie asked why I would want to do that, I shook my head and said, "It's a long story."

At my grandmother's house, the Infant of Prague stood on top of the large console television. He wore flowing, ornate robes that my grandmother rotated according to the church calendar. He was protected by a plastic sleeve, a sort of half-circle of stiff, clear material, trimmed in gold piping like a halo encasing him. We had an Infant at home as well, also encased in that plastic sleeve, but no one came near him. He sat on a shelf gathering dust, watching us from the safety of the fireplace mantel in his sterile, dustproof perch while we played in the living room.

MY COLLEGE CLASS IN PSYCHOLOGY FUL-filled a general education requirement. Like every other college sophomore who took a Psych 101 class, I was able to diagnose myself with complete incompetence but utter confidence. My problem, I decided one day, was that I had low self-esteem. I did not think enough of myself.

I went about building up my self-esteem. I tried to give myself positive affirmations. I wrote flattering things about myself in my journals. When I went out, I walked with confidence borrowed from a bank account I did not have, going out on limbs, taking on adventures I'd have avoided in the past for fear of disappointing someone. I changed outfits with my mood like the Infant of Prague, measuring out the liturgical year from behind the safety of that protective plastic sleeve, always keeping myself just out of reach of injury, drawing fuzzy lines around myself. I felt crazy and fragmented, absolutely unsure of who I was or where I was going.

The move to Chicago with my band at the end of that summer meant I was able to pick up the threads of myself that I still liked and weave them into someone new, responsible, and adventurous, a perfect storm of the punk rock girl and the confused college sophomore who had been clawing her way around the campus in Dayton, Ohio. I promised myself that this new version of me—band member, songwriter, Columbia College writing major—was not held by the old fuzzy boundaries.

I got a job at a mortgage lender to fill in the gaps of my student loan and grants, to be able to buy groceries and cigarettes and to pay the rent. I was a student and a loan processor, a singer, a chain smoker, and a poet. I was a lapsed Catholic and a junk food addict and a seeker and a mystic, and I had just gotten into a serious relationship with a man much older than myself, the son of an unrepentant alcoholic who gave me the attention my "daddy issues" required. I did everything I could to keep the plates spinning in the many disparate and dysfunctional parts of my life, keeping everyone happy, keeping everyone calm, keeping everyone content because I was afraid of the wrestling, afraid of the fight. And in the process my own sense of self shrank again, until it was small enough to place in plastic and put high on a shelf for protection.

Every embarrassing or awkward moment I've experienced is seared into my memory. I collect these moments, I hold them inside, catalogued it seems, for easy access in any given moment. For example, I remember that day in the sixth grade getting ready for gym in the coed classroom. The girls would wear shorts under the uniform skirt, and the boys would take off their white button-down shirts to show their gym clothes. It was not until I had unbuttoned and unzipped my skirt and was in the process of bending over to drop it, by habit, by repetition really, that I remembered I'd forgotten to wear my shorts. My face was hot while I pulled the skirt back on quickly, looking around to see if anyone had noticed. I remember stupid comments I've made to perfect strangers. I remember the hurtful actions I've taken with my friends, the secrets I didn't keep, the bad-mouthing done behind someone's back, the bad advice, the unanswered letter and missed birthday.

Regret is a terrible roommate. I stab myself in the heart daily with "I wish I hadn't" after losing my temper or giving into tempting thoughts or too many glasses of wine or saying too much about another person. I don't forget my transgressions. I pile them up in my psyche, locked behind French doors in that side parlor where I can see them. I can't go a day without remembering the regret, worrying that I am not forgiven, contemplating whom else I may have injured.

Regret is the roommate I pay to stay with me. Often I think about kicking it out. It doesn't contribute to the household. It never cleans up after itself. It eats all my food and drinks all the best scotch. It never sleeps, it always whispers, always sighs when I make new promises; it hates my friends, and it hates me. I often wonder, if my regret hates me so much, why do I keep it around? The simplest answer I can muster is that I'm afraid of making that mistake again; I'm afraid the damage is too deep, too strong for an apology to heal. I'm afraid that whatever I've said or done has become rooted in that relationship so that everything we do together going forward is forever tinged with my errors. I am not good enough. I am not strong enough. I am not forgiven. I put myself in purgatory for embarrassing and awkward moments.

"LET THEM FIGHT." DAVE AND I SAW CHRIS-topher Miller when we got back to Chicago. We'd been seeing him as our counselor since before we were married. We'd often joke that we were just paying him to be our best and wisest friend. Even if that was true, it was worth it. Chris was the only person I'd met who could, in the face of my anxieties and issues, say things like, "You know, Jesus had issues with his family of origin too," without them sounding trite or dismissive. When he said things like this, it always hit me square in the jaw, and I'd nod my head, putting that together like the tumblers on a safe falling into place.

We trusted him, so when we came back to Chicago we sought him out again to figure out our lives in the wake of our time in Nashville, our struggles with parenting, and the divide that was opening up between us around religion. Most of the session was about our boys and their own wrestling—in play, in anger, in boredom; they wrestled physically and emotionally all day long, and it was wearing me down.

When one boy would complain that the other was hitting him, I'd go to my forward position of non-violence, going Jesus-like as I pressed my thumbs and fingers together and instructed them to breathe and take a moment, then to turn the other cheek. No matter how I drilled the concepts of "treat oth-ers the way you want to be treated" and "do not retaliate" into them, it always turned ugly. When I forbade their even touching each other in a given situation, they'd sit on their time-out couches and say hateful things to each other, goading each other and drawing tears once again.

We were out of ideas, so we asked Chris Miller about this. "Let them fight," he said.

My inner Gandhi cleared his throat and shook his head as I responded, "What?"

"Let them fight." He said that like bear cubs, sometimes boys just had to engage in the struggle. He said that sometimes the only way for them to communicate, to find their way and to earn respect for one another, would be to just let them wrestle their way through it. "Give them permission to fight back when they're attacked."

In that moment I weighed all that my pacifist tendencies had taught me against all that my time with Christopher Miller had taught me, and though it grieved me, I put my trust in Dr. Miller. With great fear and trembling, the next time one boy hit the other and the injured party came to me for assistance, I choked back my inner Gandhi and told my son to fight back. The look on the faces of all three boys was shock and awe. With raised eyebrows, they looked at each other and slowly filed out of the room. I got out the bandaids and the antiseptic spray and prayed as I waited for them to learn to work it out on their own. And they did, over time, with noise and injury and first aid, and then healing.

I AM CONVINCED NOW THAT FOR AS LONG as I see my journey from the safety of the mantelpiece, wrapped in the protective clear vinyl sleeve and dressed in the finery of the day, I will always find fault, point fingers, and feel the lacking. I often see myself standing there apart from the whole world, trying to bring about the peace and calm I feel sure will finally tip me over the edge toward being a better version of myself. If only I had more alone time, if only I had that next book on spiritual devotion, if only I had made it to this service or that confession, then I'd be more patient, more pious, more penitent.

I want to already be better, already more calm in the face of chaos, already more peaceful in the face of anger. But the more I try to channel that, the more I try to rise above and summon that peace, that calm, that sense of self, the more the fall into failure is certain. This faith thing is messy. It is most often a noisy, muddy struggle at this point, and I am the bear cub, working it out with all I have—arms grasping, legs kicking, torso twisting, heart holding out for healing. It's all necessary.

Sometimes, the wrestling is the thing.

CHAPTER 5

STATIONS

(on rest areas and roadwork)

This is a strange life, incomprehensible to the secular world; everything in it is paradox, everything is in a form opposite to the order of the secular world, and it is impossible to explain it in words. The only way to understand it is to perform the will of God, that is, to follow the commandments of Christ; the path, indicated by Him.

—St. Silouan the Athonite

It's always something.

—Roseanne Roseannadanna

It was warm that day in Miss Gardner's classroom. In an effort to save some time, Father Boyle gathered all three of our second-grade classes into one room, and we sat there, pressed together and listening. I was near the back, hiding in the corner but positioned so that I could see and hear Father Boyle. I took note of how bulbous and red his nose appeared. When he was on a roll with his speech about the Stations of the Cross, his cheeks would flush and his voice would soar. He was our pastor and our favorite priest. The rousing sixty-something Irishman was an old Navy man, and he would begin announcements in the mornings with "Now hear this! Now hear this!" and we would all giggle. No one could resist Father Boyle.

That afternoon he spoke of the night Christ died. He spoke of the Creed we'd say each Wednesday morning at Mass, that He "suffered, died, and was buried." This was our lesson for the day. He used the words he'd repeat during the Mass, "a death He freely accepted . . ." he continued, and I began to cry. I sat in the back of the room hearing that Christ "freely accepted" his death, shaking and afraid, unsure of why anyone would choose death.

Father Boyle spared no details of that death. His bones were crushed as nails were pounded into His already tortured and beaten body. He told us Christ died most likely from asphyxiation, that His lungs would not have been able to function, and that the air would be forced from Him and not returned with every labored breath. He told us of the words Christ shouted from the cross, "It is finished!" and I got light-headed.

I put my head against the yellow-painted cinderblock wall, my cheek pressed against the cold, dusty surface, and I broke into a sweat. "A death He freely accepted," I heard in my ears, and the room was spinning. I closed my eyes and leaned into the wall. When I opened my eyes, what seemed like hours later, everyone was starting to stand up. The boy next to me said I had fallen asleep. I was shaking and dizzy. It was the first time I fainted and no one knew.

THE ORTHODOX TRADITION DOES NOT offer Stations of the Cross. As I toured Holy Trinity Church in Nashville during my catechism classes, I noticed the absence of the stations. The Stations of the Cross at St. Teresa were spread along the walls, circling the massive stone sanctuary. They stood at grownup eye level and depicted the various stages of the Passion of Christ.

The stations show the arrest and condemnation of Jesus. They show Him carrying the heavy timber cross to Golgotha and then falling under the weight of that cross. The stations show Him meeting His mother, then Simeon and Veronica on the road, falling again and then again, in the sight of those who loved Him. They show the nails pounding into His hands and His feet, spilling blood and sparing breath until at last He died, his body taken down and laid in a tomb.

The Station I had always loved best was Veronica wiping the face of Jesus. The lore was that after she wiped His face, the cloth was miraculously stained with an imprint of Jesus' face. St. Veronica went on to become a martyr. Maybe it was never Veronica who bore that cloth but some other woman, nameless and unknown; in any case, Veronica got the credit. It helps to have a name and a story and a bit of cloth to cling to when we're uncertain the event took place at all.

The church becomes dark during the Stations of the Cross, and with each Station I saw more than the pictures on the wall, heard more than the words spoken by the priest, felt more than boredom or disgust. Each time we practiced the Stations of the Cross, I felt all those events brush against the surface of my skin. It was so real, so vivid a picture that a veil would cover my brain and my head would buzz. My face would flush, then drain of blood as I imagined the nails going into the palms, the side split open spilling blood and water, until unconsciousness would take me over.

The feeling of my head hitting the cold marble floor of St. Teresa of Avila Church in Cincinnati, Ohio, became familiar, my own personal religious practice. I passed out so many times in church while I was in grade school that eventually no one wanted to stand next to me during Mass, let alone during the Stations of the Cross. The teachers would make me sit on the end of the pew near the door. If I started to look green, they would open the door to let in a breeze. No one wanted to have to carry a sweaty fifth-grader outside while the priest processed through the church.

Standing in Holy Trinity the first time during Vespers, I felt that old familiar church-related flush of face. The rain was coming down heavily that night, and I had no raincoat, no umbrella, nowhere to go. It always seems to be the rain that holds me captive. It had been a long time since I attended a church with all the elements I'd come to associate with passing out during a service: the pews, the long times of standing, the smell of the incense, the repetition of the words, hammering the tender skin of my cheeks, and the headache starting just above my temples.

I could always tell when a fainting spell was coming on. It was like standing on a balcony rail: I would teeter on the edge as the blood drained from my face, close my eyes, and surrender to the loss of consciousness. But here, there was no blood trigger, no description of the nails in hands and side pierced. Standing in Holy Trinity the first time during Vespers brought me right back to the Stations of the Cross, the most vulnerable I had ever been in church, surrendering time after time to the hard marble floor in an act of unconscious performance art, embracing it all with full and complete sweaty abandon.

Mr. Rotter taught English Lit my senior year. Like Father Boyle, years earlier, he was a rabid storyteller, relishing gory details wherever he could find them as we studied Chaucer's *Canterbury Tales*. The work itself is visceral and meaty, and Mr. Rotter's ability to translate the Old English terminology was profound. It was a brilliantly painted portrait for the modern Catholic teenage girl.

It was the bloodletting that got to me. I'd skipped breakfast; lunch was at least an hour away. Mr. Rotter described the historical practices of leeches and bloodletting and associated them with the language of Chaucer, the meanings behind the references, but in general, the physiological reality of the cut and then the blood spilling out. Grace Gill sat next to me taking notes, and when I turned to face the window, hoping for a breeze, her eyes were wide as she told me I looked terrible.

I woke as Mr. Rotter was waving people away from me with the familiar "give her air" line floating into my ears. The nurse arrived at the classroom with a wheelchair, and she called my mother when we reached her office. The sweat was beginning to dry on my face, cementing lines on my cheeks from the streaks of failed eyeliner. When my mother arrived, she took me to the doctor, who recommended a neurological workup. So my mother took me next to the hospital, where I was admitted. It was my seventeenth birthday.

"Now we have come to the setting of the sun . . ." The storm cooled the narthex through the open wooden doors of Holy Trinity while I listened to the words of the priest at Vespers. I stood at the back of the church, looking out at my car in the driving rain, then looking back into the sanctuary. I found my way to the restroom by trial and error and stared at my face in the mirror, color returning as I congratulated myself on avoiding the fainting spell. I fixed my eye makeup and took some deep breaths, wondering if anyone in the small group who were present had noticed me standing there colorless, leaving in a cold sweat, breathing deeply, then returning.

Vespers was a short service, and I'd spent most of it worried about my head hitting the marble floor. But I moved quietly to the back row again and sat down discreetly, pretending to follow along in the book, pretending to know why I was there at all instead of at home with my family. I felt nauseated and uncomfortable and unprotected. I felt vulnerable, and so I sat in the back row and waited there for the rain to end.

THE ANGLICAN CHURCH WE ATTENDED FOR a while in Nashville was pastored by a friend of ours. It was our third church down South, not counting the failed attempt at yet another church plant. When the Wellspring disintegrated in a mist of confusion and doubt, disagreements in power structure, personality clashes, and financial considerations, we started showing up at the Redeemer in Nashville.

I went alone at first, because I needed something and I was not sure how to name it. The kids were still small, and I was stinging from the church plant failure. My abandonment issues had assaulted me full force, and Dave was already talking about moving home to Chicago. Moving home felt like moving backward, and though I was injured from the string of religious, cultural, and interpersonal upsets, there were still friendships I'd built and I didn't want to leave yet. So I dug my heels into Nashville.

Eventually, I did bring the kids to church, and Dave came along, falling asleep in the pew more often than not. I was both puzzled and a little impressed that he could manage to fall asleep week after week as we sat there. He'd drop off within seconds of the sermon starting, and if I let him go, he'd start snoring quietly a few minutes after that. I threatened to make him sit in the front row so Fr. Thomas would see him, but I never followed through. I considered it an act of defiance, thumbing his nose at the institution of religion, one more rebellion on the road of faith, and I was angry with him about it.

"PAPA" WAS MY MOTHER'S FATHER, MARRIED to my grandmother, whom we called "Muzzie." Papa carried candy in his pockets, and he called us girls his "whiffenpoofs." He was famous for doing things like sewing my brother's cloth diaper together once when he was watching us, because he couldn't find the diaper pins. In my fuzzy memories of him, he is tall and handsome. He is warm and caring and regal.

I was standing in the kitchen near the avocado green wall phone when it rang, and I stood there while my mother answered it and received the news that her father was dead. Papa's heart attack was sudden and definitive. He was driving on a busy road, and when the heart attack took hold of him, he pulled over and parked the car on the side. Blinkers flashing, he slumped over the wheel and left the world as traffic raced by. An exhale into the storm, and he was gone. The policeman who found him said his decision to pull over was probably heroic; if he'd continued like that—as many might, trying to get one more place, arrive at one more destination—he might have driven into traffic and taken someone else with him.

I was seven when he died.

WHEN THINGS WERE DESPERATE WHEN I was young and the phone rang near dinnertime, my mother would have my brother or me answer it. "If it's for me, tell them

I'm in the bathroom," she would instruct. When this tactic failed over time, she would instruct us to say she was not home. Even at ten years old, I knew from their tone if the caller was a bill collector. I would pretend to write the name and the phone number, sometimes drawing it out as I pretended to find a pen and paper while they waited. I used my best kid voice and my most innocent responses, hoping they were laced with secret messages: "Don't shut off our electricity." "Don't take our house."

I confessed little white lies each week. They were venial sins, sins that would condemn us in Purgatory but not send us directly to Hell. At night when things were quiet, I would pray for our family; I would cry from my fear. I still prayed for the departed souls of my grandfather, Papa, and my great-grandmother, Ma. I would do the math in my head night after night, trying to figure out how much longer they might have to spend in what I visualized as a great train station somewhere between Heaven and Hell. Their tickets would be time-stamped to show the balance between their character and their venial sins.

Papa was a good man; kind and generous, with a wide smile and open arms, he kept candy in his pocket because of his blood sugar problems, but I always like to think he kept candy in his pocket for us, as a secret treat. Ma was my grandmother's mother on my mom's side. My memory of her is limited to the stories we told, to the pictures I saw, and to the slim recollection of her holding me on her lap during her last years, my first years.

When I was seventeen, I was still praying for the soul of

my grandfather. As I understood it, Purgatory was a rest stop on the way to Heaven, one last station before the end. One's time in Purgatory was related to how one spent one's time on earth, but I had no way to gauge time as God knew it, and no way to know sin as God knew it. The mechanics were fuzzy, but I prayed for his soul in Purgatory for as long as I attended Mass regularly, because I loved and missed him. Though I could not bear to think of Papa stuck in the waiting room for Heaven, in some ways I imagined him there, patient and content, giving out candy and making conversation with the people around him. It made him feel closer to me, as if I could still touch the buttons on his clean, stiff dress shirt and feel the bristles of his mustache when he kissed my cheek.

BY EASTER OF THE SECOND YEAR WE attended Redeemer in Nashville, Dave was finished with regular attendance at church again. He was feeling the pressure of work, still active in Chicago, which meant he spent half his time there and half in the middle of nowhere with us. He was feeling the pressure of the leadership power struggles that had come up within a small men's ministry he'd begun. He was feeling the pressure of the mortgage, and the weight gain that came with stress and parenting four small chaos-makers, and tensions with me, and religion and anger, and the bouts of vertigo that had caused him to cut a work trip short.

He lay sprawled on the couch that Holy Saturday as I led a workshop with a friend in the morning. The doctor was trying to cure the vertigo with a medicinal "reset" cocktail along with rest to restore the inner ear fluid balance. Dave spent most of the day watching a four-hour documentary film about monks called *Into Great Silence*. Every time I walked through the room he was sleeping or groggy, his snoring accompanied by the silence or the chanting or the shuffling along of the Carthusian monks of the Grande Chartreuse, high in the French Alps.

We both thought the chest pains he'd been having all week were muscle spasms, brought on by the hard work he'd done in getting the pool opened, his arms reaching forward over and over, pulling back the winter veil, reaching and releasing, lifting and falling with the weight of the water. By three o'clock that day, Dave couldn't take the pain or the dizziness anymore. My mother, who was visiting, saw his pale, sweaty skin and insisted I take him to the hospital.

The walk-in clinic wouldn't even let us past the sign-in sheet. The moment the receptionist put together the color of Dave's skin with the words "chest pain" on the white paper, she directed us down the road to the emergency room. We laughed a little, but her face remained serious. She shook her head and instructed us to go immediately to the ER.

We'd made this our first stop, thinking a torn ligament would be the diagnosis and muscle relaxants would be the prescription. It was a way to avoid the hours-long wait that always came with an ER visit. But we were turned away into the rainy Holy Saturday afternoon. We moved to the car as quickly as we could to beat the gathering power of the storm and drove down the road to the hospital named for St. Thomas, the doubter, the one who needed proof of the Resurrection.

We signed in, Dave making sure to put in an appearance at the window in the hope that his complexion might speed things up, and apparently it did just that. He was taken back immediately and hooked up to the heart monitor. We still laughed a little, thinking we'd put something over on them, getting in so quickly with a packed waiting room. The monitor showed nothing spectacular at first, and we felt vindicated. They took blood to be sure they could rule out a heart event, and Dave lobbied to go home, promising to see his regular doctor on Monday. He lobbied with the ER doc and the nurses, and even his own physician by phone, but no one would let him go. His age, his physical condition, his history, and his symptoms worked against the idea, and so, begrudgingly, he stayed.

The first blood test to detect the proteins that might be released in the case of a heart attack was negative. It was already late in the day, and I was making the long drive home to get Dave some things for his overnight stay, angry to have Easter interrupted for a torn muscle. I reached the house, packed the bag, kissed the kids, and finished the Easter baskets for the following morning, then made the return trip to the hospital.

The second set of test results came in when I reached the hospital; they showed protein in the blood. The EKG was beginning to show some changes then, and they prepped Dave and took him to the operating room before I realized what it all meant. He was still in good spirits; we both thought it was crazy, and I didn't worry. There was no clutching at the chest, no pulling over to the side of the road and drifting to the next station.

They call the left anterior descending artery "the widow-maker," and Dave's was ninety percent blocked. They call it this because when it is blocked, it produces little to no sign of heart attack when a coronary event comes along. The artery blockage had been starving Dave's heart for a long time, explaining the forgetfulness, the crankiness, the constant napping from exhaustion. They caught it at just the right moment. If he'd gone home, he might have died that night, quietly, slipping off into great silence.

I realized then that every story, every miracle, every breath taken by followers and friends and family, they are all stations on the line, the progression from one place to another—not just places on the road, but places of the heart and of the spirit and of the journey. These are all the Stations of the Cross.

"LORD, NOW LETTEST THOU THY SERVANT depart in peace . . ." The rain was still pouring outside Holy Trinity when Vespers ended with the priest speaking the final words of the service. I was still sitting in the back row, looking around the sanctuary at the progression of icons housed by nearly every wall surface, all the saints and martyrs facing in toward us, watching and waiting as I watched and as I waited. St. John Chrysostom peered at me from the left, St. Anna from the right; John the Baptist stared out from the iconostasis at the front of the sanctuary. They were all stations, all stops on the dusty road before me.

The rain pounded outside when I turned to leave, the sky still black and laced with lightning, and I watched as the small group of worshippers filed out, stopping to venerate the icon of Christ, retrieving umbrellas and smiling with a nod to me. A young woman offered to share her umbrella with me, and I shook my head. "It'll let up," I said. "It can't rain this hard and last."

I stared into the storm and knew I would have to make a run for it finally. I found the idea of it no longer bothered me. The rain on my face might even feel good after my sweaty brush with fainting. I had already won the battle with unconsciousness today. The storm didn't scare me anymore.

CHAPTER 6

ROUTINE

(on laundry, liturgy, and women's work)

*Laundry, liturgy and women's work all serve to ground us
in the world, and they need not grind us down. Our daily
tasks, whether we perceive them as drudgery or essential,
life-supporting work, do not define who we are as women
or as human beings.*

—Kathleen Norris

*I'm a housewife: I spend far more time on housework than
anything else.*

—Annie Dillard

I'm kind of a housewife now. I realized this as I drove the
kids to their gymnastics class. For all my liberal and fem-
inistic leanings, for all my spouting about ambition and
rebellion and punk rock, I am kind of a housewife now.

When my second child was born, I was still producing films, commercials, and the occasional industrial video with my husband. I was taking calls in the loft office across the hall from our living space. I was nursing while typing up scripts and projecting budgets and booking camera crews, praying the baby would not start crying or a client would not drop by without notice. The office hummed along while I juggled parenting and paperwork poorly.

It became clear a few months in that even though our daughter was in preschool most of the day and the baby was sleeping most of the day, my sleep-deprived brain and the compromises I had to make were taking a toll on me and on my work. I felt crazy all the time. I was cranky and bitter and mean, and so I quit my job, mostly. As years and children were added to the equation, I let go more and more of the work I'd been doing and turned toward the work that pressed in on me in a real and tangible way. If I did not write every day, I could find little evidence of that loss, but if I did not feed and clothe the four children, if I did not clean the bathroom, if I did not empty the trashcan, the effect was immediate and my traveling companions were vocal about it. And so I'm kind of a housewife now, and it bothers me a little.

Sweeping and mopping the floor every night before bed was a ritual, becoming a ritual the way things do, not so much because of the intention but because of the daily practice of it, the necessity of it. After the kids were in bed and maybe nearly sleeping, I'd load the dishwasher and run hot water into the sink.

Having four children under the age of six meant the floors were always dirty from bare feet and mud fights and finger painting and food thrown, dropped, and discarded. Baths sometimes went untaken and clothes were unlaundered, bathrooms were passable, but the kitchen floor had to be clean and the sink had to be clear.

Those were the quotidian tasks done, the daily prayers said. Without that I would have no hope in the morning. If sticky floors had greeted me in the morning on my way to the coffee maker, I might never have survived another day. With a clean and clear sink I could imagine I was keeping my motherly head above water, just above water, and so no matter how tired I was after the bedtime wrestling match with the kids, I went to the kitchen and began my own bedtime ritual, which consisted not of Oil of Olay but Murphy's Oil Soap. I pushed aside worrying about my own skin for the sake of my sanity. It was calming and orderly in an otherwise chaotic life.

There was something about letting the water rush over my hands as I rinsed the dishes, placing the cups and glasses neatly in between the prongs of the upper rack as I filled the dishwasher. There was something about the clean water in the sink slowly shifting, showing the wear of the day transferring from the floor to the mop to the water. It was the least I could do to keep from drowning.

MY SISTER WAS ONLY ABOUT SIX WHEN MY insomnia first kicked up. I liked the nighttime because it was quiet and I could think. I had my best ideas in the middle of the night. I'd lie there wide awake in my bed, staring at the ceiling, staring at the window, staring at my hands in the light of the streetlamp and sometimes the moon.

I had been reading about brownies, which in folklore were a little like hobgoblins except that they helped out around the house, usually in the dead of night because they did not want to be seen. I was reading about brownies because I had just joined the Girl Scouts and at my age, we were named Brownies for the fairy folk. Brownies would do housework in exchange for food or sweets, and they usually made their home in an unused part of the house.

Since I liked to nap and play during the day under my bed and in my closet, and because I liked to clean and had insomnia at night, I felt some kinship with the brownies, and so I got the idea to clean at night, when my parents were asleep. I wanted to help out. I wanted my mom to have a break, and so I snuck around my dimly lit bedroom and picked up whatever I could, as quietly as I could.

I woke up my sister the next night, explaining with some quiet enthusiasm this plan to help Mom. She complied, willing but unmotivated. She helped for a few minutes before her tiredness took over, and so I let her go back to bed. I think I was lonely, I was looking for a way to be helpful and to occupy my overworked and worried brain, and I didn't want to be alone in that worry. She still mentions this practice to me. She does not remember it as fondly as I do, and I do remember it fondly. That late-night housekeeping was a way for me to keep from worrying. It was a saving grace to feel as though there was something I could do to help, something within my small and delicate grasp.

MY DAD OPENED THE BIG FAMILY BIBLE we kept on the shelf next to the *Lives of the Saints* book series. It was musty and it creaked when the binding was tried. He flipped through the pages as we sat around him on the couch; my mother was in a chair across the small living room. I remember the couch pattern, the feel of the texture, waffled and rough, but I cannot remember the chair, only my mother's face as my dad paged through the heavy golden Bible.

He'd never called us all into the living room for this before. In my memory he'd never opened that Bible. But I had. I would sit in the corner of that room, on the floor, in front of the built-in bookcases that framed the decorative fireplace. I sat next to the five-foot statue of the Sacred Heart of Jesus that my dad had gotten from a Catholic hospital that was closing. My dad always seemed to hear about these buildings being torn down, whether it was from his co-workers or his many brothers, and he found a way to "scrounge," as he called it.

The day he came home with the Sacred Heart statue he rushed into the house, excited. He told my mom he had a surprise in the car but he needed help getting it out. His younger brother, Chuck, came by and helped him remove the statue from the back of the truck he'd borrowed to obtain the treasure. In the process of moving it, they'd managed to bump it badly enough to crack the plaster around a number of the fingers, something that disturbed my dad because, of course, the statue was blessed. It was sacred. Catholic artifacts, such as statues that are blessed, cannot be thrown into a dump somewhere. Anything blessed in the Catholic tradition must be either buried or burned. My dad had saved this statue from being burned or buried and saved the hospital administrators some hassles in the process.

The statue stood taller than most of us kids and resided in that quiet corner of the room, keeping watch over the bookcase and the dinner table. Because of the rough ride into the house, he was missing a few fingers on his right hand, leaving only the thick wire hanging from his forward-facing hand. I had to be careful when I sat on the metal register beneath those wires to keep from having them scrape my scalp.

I would wedge myself beneath his injured hand with the gilded family Bible and run my fingers over the outside of that book. I would hold my face close to the pages to take in the smell, and I would read the names written in the front, names of our family. When my dad opened the book as we gathered around him on the couch, he told us we should pray together as a family every night after dinner. He said he would read a Bible story and we could talk about it. It was my first exposure to what I'd understand later was a "family Bible study."

That night we fidgeted and whined in the eyesight of the Sacred Heart of Jesus, but not too much. It was new and we were eager to hear from our dad. He was so often absent, so often unavailable. We swam in the attention when it came, but my Dad's family Bible study only lasted a few nights. We were so young, grade school at best. It was new, and my mother and father were exhausted parenting the four of us, fighting my dad's post-traumatic stress disorder, which was at that time still undiscovered. It was the giant in the road all the time, and we did not know how to get around it. Every effort just stopped until we fumbled through it, throwing rocks at that giant's enormous sandals and shouting with our tiny voices.

We hoped we were better for it; we took the failures as a kind of victorious defeat because we were all still alive. We'd try again, something else, something new, another healthy eating plan, another family time adventure, and in it would be some kernel of goodness, some kernel of truth. I found it sitting on the floor under that five-foot statue of the Sacred Heart of Jesus with fingers broken down to wire, while I paged through that enormous golden book that creaked when the binding was tried. I found it, though I did not recognize it at the time.

When I was young I never thought about leaving home. I was focused on keeping home together, keeping us together. All that energy spent on family time, conversation, and that golden-bound Bible on the coffee table yielded only more fragmentation. My dad continued to float away, and our family continued to tear at its own bindings. We drifted and we tore and we regrouped in the container of the everyday pace of our lives. We played soccer, we attended Mass, we played in the yard with the neighbors until the sun went down. Our uniforms were pressed, our shirts were laundered, our lunches were packed.

We were creatures of habit because without that habit, without that schedule, without that structure we were falling apart at the seams, pages floating off into the dark and uncharted waters.

But now, my family, this family I've built with my husband, shirks routine. It shakes off the structure our families of origin used for stability. We are rocket-powered. We are jet-fueled. We are space-age and internet savvy, and even as it powers us, it drains us, too. Somewhere inside of me, when the structure and the schedule and the demands of becoming Orthodox call out, I find myself frozen by anxiety. I am afraid to be pigeonholed and held accountable. I am distressed and guilt-ridden, and then I ask myself why I even bother at all.

And then I remember that I am kind of a housewife now, and that it is so often the routine that saves me in the middle of the chaos. I remember that it is the small moments and simple gestures, the stolen time with musty books under the hand of the Sacred Heart of Jesus, the quiet of the night picking up socks from the floor while everyone sleeps, the murmured prayers in the carpool pickup and the grocery store and the Vespers services. These are the quotidian things, the daily things, the essential things that hold us together when everything else feels as though it's drifting out of reach.

CHAPTER 7

FIRE AND ICE

(on taking sides)

*The great and merciful surprise is that we come to God not
by doing it right but by doing it wrong!*

—Richard Rohr

My grandmother's kitchen smelled like bleach on a
rainy day. She never cooked. Apart from the store-
bought cinnamon rolls she heated for us the morning she remarried, I do not remember her ever cooking in that
kitchen.

I was staying the night with her for the first time. I slept in
the king-size bed, on the side left vacant after my grandfather
died. He had been gone for several years by then. His side of

the bed was next to the window, and outside the window were the front porch and the lazy residential street of Coronado Avenue. I lay awake that night listening to my grandmother's heavy snore while I peered out the window through the gauzy curtain at the streetlight and beyond that, the trees waving in the wind.

It has always taken me a long time to get to sleep. At bedtime, ideas, songs, words, and dreams would all buzz in my head for what seemed like hours every night. I would try to talk with my sister, but it was as though her pillow contained a sleep agent that mine was missing. The moment she lay down she was out. Some nights my sister would talk in her sleep, and I would perk up and try to carry on the conversation, happy for the company, but it never worked out that way. It was a one-way radio. I was only overhearing a conversation she was having with someone else, an idea, a song, a dream. I was not invited into that conversation.

The morning of my grandmother's wedding to Bill, she heated those store-bought cinnamon rolls in a bun warmer that Papa, my grandfather, had purchased years before. It plugged into the wall and looked as though it had never been used. She heated the appliance and then opened it, placing each frosting-covered roll carefully in the tray. She would lick her fingers when frosting spilled onto them; she smacked her lips together as she worked at it, as the frosting leaked out over the edges of the bun warmer. She seemed younger than I'd ever seen her in that moment. Muzzie was the grand matriarch of the Thompson family, always impeccably dressed and wearing full makeup with her hair done. Seeing her like this in her robe, barefaced and hair matted, licking her fingers and her lips and smiling like a small girl, was a shock to me. I was entranced witnessing her in that unguarded moment.

"If you're not with me, you're against me." When I was fourteen my mother and father separated. We were living in Muzzie's house by then, the house my mother had lived in when she was a child. Muzzie and Grandpa Bill had moved into an apartment because of his failing health, and they'd offered the family home on Coronado Avenue to us for a good price a few years earlier. We'd outgrown our house on Loretta.

This was even closer to school for us; it was so close my older brother and I could come home for lunch in grade school. Because my mother had gone back to college at that time, she would often be in class when we'd arrive home around noon, so JD and I would open cans of Campbell's soup on our own, heating it on the electric stove or in bowls in the microwave.

When my dad told me they were separating and probably divorcing, he was sitting at the dining room table, making notes on a yellow legal pad. He looked sad and resigned. He'd already been sleeping on a cot in the basement, but now he would be getting an apartment in the neighborhood. I imagined him in a one-room shack, eating Campbell's soup from the can with only a bare light bulb hanging from the dingy water-stained ceiling.

At that time, the late seventies and early eighties, being a divorced Catholic on the west side of Cincinnati, Ohio, was a stigma. It affected the condition of one's soul, not to mention one's stature in the parish. My parents, who had been active in the church, readers and ushers and lay eucharistic ministers, were no longer asked to participate. Being a divorced Catholic was shaming to the entire family, and our grand matriarch was not pleased. I'm sure there were many conversations between my mother and her mother; I'm sure there were angry words and tears. In the end Muzzie refused to speak to my mother, and she refused to see us.

For three years they did not speak and we did not see our grandmother. It was not for lack of trying on my mother's part. My grandmother was a cedar. She was strong and majestic; she could not be moved once she planted herself. Three years found us living blocks away from Muzzie and never seeing her or speaking with her on the phone. It was strangely undiscussed among my cousins and myself. Perhaps it is because it was not without precedent. My grandmother had a habit of disowning anyone unfaithful to her way of thinking. She often spouted her self-assigned adage: "If you're not with me, you're against me." I didn't know what it meant until it happened to my mother, and when it happened to my mother it happened to us all.

I still loved my grandmother in that time even though we were not together. Thankfully, I was not asked to choose between them. That choice was made for me. If I had been asked to choose, I could only have chosen my mother. There was no question. I walked the wide road in between my mother and my grandmother knowing I could not solve their issues, even though I wanted to be able to do so. I knew that my grandmother might come around eventually, the cedar bending because of time or a strong wind. I still loved her, and I still wished for her. I loved most that version of her in the kitchen, her hair askew, licking her lips and her fingertips as we waited for the cinnamon rolls to heat.

My parents never asked us to take sides in their divorce. Things were messy and confusing, and we often chose sides anyway. My older brother lived with my dad for a short time during his last year in high school, but my dad lived just around the corner, so we still saw both of them all the time. The chasm that existed between my parents was deep; it had been eroding like water through the Grand Canyon from almost the start of their relationship. When they said they were divorcing, it came as no shock to us, and so rather than lament what we would be missing, my siblings and I simply lived in where we were at that moment.

It was easier to love my Dad when we weren't busy being resentful that he was absent without leave from our family. It was easier to love my mom when she wasn't distraught or angry with my dad, and so we didn't choose sides. We did not have the energy for it. We lived life as if we were in a batting cage and we took each pitch as it came, one at a time. It was the best we could do, and it helped us to navigate the transitions.

WHEN I ASKED FATHER GREGORY ABOUT my homosexual friends, he was taken aback for a moment. I did not want to be told I had to choose sides, because choosing sides about who was right and who was wrong made the issue black and white, fire and ice. In my history and in my experience, it meant I would have to be against someone, and I was not willing to do that.

I'd gone into his cramped office with a list in my hand. The items on the list were my deal-breakers. I thought they were the "I cannot be Orthodox" items. I went into that meeting with a list and a "check yes or no" box in my head. Can I be Orthodox if I have tattoos? Can I be Orthodox if I go to yoga class at the gym? Can I be Orthodox if I choose not to judge my gay friends?

It was a defiant stance, and I asked each question with a clenched fist. That fist was never meant for striking, though. That fist was curled around my poor, suffering heart. That fist was armor around an injury, and the real questions I wanted to ask were, "Will you let me in if I have tattoos?" and "Will you let me in if I go to yoga classes?" and "Will you let me in if I choose love over judgment?" Do I have to choose sides? Will you let me in?

A few years after Muzzie's self-imposed exclusion from our lives, my mom decided to call her. We had been out buying a dress for my senior prom, an event I had to talk my punk-rock college-age boyfriend into attending at all. A neighbor was cutting down a tree that ran down the middle of the fence in our yard, a tree that had been there since before my mother was born. My mother called Muzzie to ask about the property line and about the tree, but she was compelled to call Muzzie for other reasons she could not explain.

The gold lamé dress hung covered in plastic on the back of my mother's bedroom door while she made the call, speaking plainly to my grandmother about the tree, as if no time had passed between their last conversation about the divorce and this one. When she had answered the questions about the tree and the fence and the property line, Muzzie mentioned she had to go into the hospital for a procedure. She did not say much about the reason. She even implied it was not serious. She just wanted us to know.

That Monday she entered the hospital to find out why she was having the symptoms. On Tuesday she was diagnosed with a particularly aggressive form of cancer. On Wednesday we visited her and I told her about my prom dress, leaving out the part about the punk-rock college-age boyfriend, and on Sunday she died.

In his office that day, Father Gregory saw me leaking out over the edges. In answer to the question about my gay friends, he said gently, "It would not be Orthodox to judge someone," and the fingers of my clenched fist relaxed a little. My poor, suffering heart pounded in my hand, grateful for the space, grateful for the room to breathe.

It was the first of many lists and many meetings and many moments of watching my fingers peel away reluctantly from my poor, suffering heart, because the answers would never be a clean "yes" or "no." It would never be that easy. Being Orthodox is not easy. It is never a clean and clear campaign of rules and regulations. It is not a set of bullet points and check-boxes, a set of sides to be chosen. Being Orthodox does not fit into "if you're not with me, you're against me." Being Orthodox is messy and beautiful and stripped down wearing no makeup, revealed and vulnerable. It finds me leaking out over the edges of the appliance as it heats, like those cinnamon rolls being warmed in my grandmother's kitchen.

CHAPTER 8

BODY AND BLOOD

(on bleeding)

All the soarings of my mind begin in my blood.
—Rainer Maria Rilke

When I was a child I prayed for the stigmata. I wanted the wounds of Christ. I would stare at my hands as I prayed and wish for them to tear open, to bleed quietly. I would think about the gloves I might wear to school to hide my affliction, to show my affliction; the flesh ripping apart at inopportune moments, fluids seeping through the white cotton covering. I would imagine the pain; now spoken, now groaning, now pressing my hands to my side in this representation of Christ and suffering, because to walk through that physical pain would mean some relief from the constant war at home.

It may not have been a stormy night, but when I write about it I always tell it that way. Whether intentional or unintentional, for effect or for comfort, I tell that the storm raged outside while my parents argued downstairs until the thunder roared, the door slammed, and my dad's car lumbered off down the road. It was about money or my dad's most recent lost job, at least on the surface. That was only the most recent injury. The real wound had been bleeding a long time; scarring, scabbing over, the stigmata our family wore on its hands, its feet, its side.

The real wound was Korea, my dad leaving my mom shortly after their wedding to join the army and the cleanup of a conflict across an ocean. The real wound was Vietnam, where he served his time as a captain, training the men of Charlie Company and then coming home only a few months before those men would, under new leadership, commit the atrocities of the Mai Lai massacre. The real wound was war. It followed him home and we did not know it was there. It bled quietly and tore open again and again with sudden, alarming frequency.

IT WAS A POET WHO FIRST PLANTED THE notion of Orthodoxy in my brain. I was attending a conference in Michigan and I was four months pregnant. Although I still wrote from time to time, writing conferences were not something I did. When my friend asked me to go with her, I surprised myself by saying "yes." I thought I was too busy. I was working as a line producer on small films and big commercials, I was raising my daughter, I was trying to have another baby. I had stopped writing poetry.

The move away from writing poetry was gradual. It was a gentle slope into a muddy pond; it was a collection of choices. There was no one thing that took the pen from my hand. Life got in the way. Poetry was an elective. I elected to let it slip into the water. I elected to let my inner poet slide into that deep water and float there a long time, until at last I could no longer see her there drowning.

That writer's conference in Michigan found me bleeding. The doctor assured me that it was normal, that the baby was fine, the heartbeat strong. Still, I was nervous. I had miscarried twice already. I did not know how to be hopeful anymore. I was afraid of hope, so instead, I sullenly chose gratitude. Each day of the pregnancy I would journal, and each entry began with, "I can't believe I'm still pregnant. Thank you, God." I was cranky and fearful, but I chose to begin each day with that acknowledgment even though each night I would go to sleep afraid, clutching my belly, talking to my baby as I drew my knees into myself as if that would keep him in, as if that would keep him alive. In the morning I was alive, he was alive, we were both resurrected. But there was little joy in that resurrection, just a steely determination to rally through, gratitude through gritted teeth, and a strong desire to stem the bleeding.

My friend Karen and I stayed with someone I had not met. I volunteered to take the inflatable mattress in her cold basement den. I wanted the seclusion. I liked the possibility that if I fell into sobbing I could bury myself in that cold room, under heavy quilts. I sat with my worry and my fear, my bleeding ebbing, flowing, unpredictable. I'd sneak to the small half bath on the first floor, being careful not to creak the stairs or floorboards, careful not to wake anyone with my well-worn worry, my emotional insomnia, my persistent sobbing. That conference found me bleeding and distant and unwilling to identify myself as injured to the strangers around me.

I don't know why I chose to hear a poet read on that first day of the conference. I did not know his work. I did not know his name. It might have been that I went on the recommendation of my friend. It could be that I went because I did not know where else to go. I drifted in and out of sessions the entire weekend. I spoke to very few people. I sat alone in dark corners and on windy benches and in cold basement dens on inflatable mattresses, and I bled.

The poet, Scott Cairns, wore his hair long, pulled back into a ponytail; he'd peer out from over his glasses now and again as he read. He had an easy voice to hear. I sat in the back with my eyes closed. I was still bleeding, in body, in spirit, in emotion. I know he spoke about becoming Orthodox and about his *chotki*—the black knotted prayer rope he wore on his wrist. I know he spoke of the Jesus Prayer, and I know he read his work, the words from "Magdalen's Epistle" breaking in, breaking the surface of the deep water to where my own drowning poet resided:

I have kissed
his feet. I have looked long

into the trouble of his face,
and met, in that intersection,
the sacred place—where body

and spirit both abide, both yield,
in mutual obsession.

BETTER THAN ANY SERMON, ANY MOTIVA-
tional talk, any therapeutic language, this poetry reached inside
of me and pulled out my drowning poet. And I knew then how
desperately I had missed her, how much I needed her here in this
moment while I was bleeding and alone. I bought his book that
day. When I got home from the conference, I bought my own
chotki online from an Orthodox monastery in Arizona. And then
I began to write poetry again, quietly, letting the words trickle
out slowly at first, then roll down the mountain in a stream, in a
river, in a flood overtaking the shores of me.

In the Orthodox tradition, women are discouraged from taking communion while they are bleeding.[1] My massage therapist
friend, Diane, told me this while she pounded the boulders in
my upper back into dust. A female client who was cradle Orthodox had told her this in passing. She asked me what I thought
of it. Diane knew me well; she'd witnessed my radical feminist
rants in our Bible study, she suffered with my suffrage-speak

---

1   This is a common, but not universal, practice among the various
    Orthodox churches.

about women in the ministry, the persistent condition of women treated as second-class citizens inside and outside the church. I argued against the popular historical position taken that women were somehow inferior, to be seen but not heard, punished by God with pain and bleeding, that constant reminder of choosing poorly in the garden.

Lying on that massage table, I rejected the assumption that she was right about this. Orthodoxy 101 had not mentioned this. None of the reading I had done nor the meetings with Father Gregory had broached this subject. I was already worried about the role of women in Orthodox practice, wondering if the Church was too old-fashioned in its approach, wondering if women were treated as equals. I had been wrestling with these female issues, and this new information was troubling. I was already struggling to understand how I would fit my history and my combat boots and my tattoos into the tradition. Maybe, I considered, there was a different version of Eastern Orthodoxy, maybe it was an ethnic quirk, maybe the Orthodox Church in America had left this particular set of rules by the side of the road before it boarded the boat to the United States.

After some research and questioning of my priest, I found that Diane was right. Orthodox, both women and men, are discouraged from taking communion while they are bleeding, regardless of the cause. This felt like a blow to my journey, a giant blocking the road. Could I be a part of a tradition that would keep me from the Body and Blood merely based upon the reality of my God-made biology?

IN THE BACK BEDROOM OF OUR HOUSE ON
Loretta Avenue, my mother taught piano lessons. She kept the
cash she earned in the top right drawer of the desk my dad
bought for her when she returned to college to finish her degree.
I don't remember her playing the piano. I only remember her
teaching. I remember the steady rhythm of the keys clacking,
the steady rhythm of the children coming and going each day
after school and sometimes on Saturday.

It was in this back bedroom that my mother first told me
about a woman's menstrual cycle. She was nervous and perhaps
a bit inarticulate about the details. I suppose, considering it now,
she got the mechanics out, but I walked away knowing only that
I would bleed. I wasn't afraid. I was curious and confused. I was
twelve.

On Superbowl Sunday three years later I finally got my
period for the first time. I'd given up the vigilant stance, the
constant wondering and being jealous of my friends who went
before me. Each time another friend started I'd express my disappointment, my fear, of being last in the crimson wave. Each
time my friends would tell me I was lucky, that I should be
glad to be spared it for so long. I didn't understand why. Even
without being told, I understood this as a rite of passage. This
will make me a woman, I thought. This is what it means to be a
woman, to leave the little girl behind and to move into the next
part of my life. I was nearly fifteen and I was afraid of being left
behind—like the thunder roaring, the door slamming, and my
dad's car lumbering off down the road.

MY FAVORITE STATUE AT ST. TERESA OF Avila Church was that of Mary, the mother of Jesus. She was situated at the front, close to the altar, near the alcove on the left side of the church. I always thought that alcove was a sitting room, a waiting area, as there were pews there and statues and relics. I wanted to sit on those seats, light those candles, watch the Mass from that angle, in the company of Mary.

In later years that alcove would be where the musicians would reside during the Mass. Mary, Queen of the Universe, stood watch over the advent of the guitar Mass in the late seventies at St. Teresa of Avila. Before it moved to the alcove in the main church, the guitar Mass began in the basement of the church, in a sort of makeshift chapel with acoustic tile ceilings and shiny linoleum flooring. The space doubled as a fellowship hall, a housing for Vacation Bible School in the summer, and a gathering place for waiting wedding parties and mothers with crying children. It was cold in the basement church but my parents preferred it to the upstairs church on Sunday mornings. The thick, black perfect-bound hymnal was absent from the guitar Mass, and in its place was a pressboard book with photocopied song sheets, lyrics only, Mother Mary blue.

Mary was ever-virgin, always wearing blue, pristine robes, and to this day when I see that color I think, "Mother Mary blue." She wore a crown of stars and at her feet was the whole earth—Queen of the Heaven, Queen of the May. I sang the "May Day" song all year round, though I was never the one chosen to crown her and she was unapproachable. She was set above us, too holy to touch, Queen of the May.

As much as I wanted to know her, I felt that we were not alike, the way I was not like the other girls in my class, not like the other women in my Protestant church communities, the other women in my grocery store line or college classes, or the other mothers at the park. Who is like me? The icon of the Theotokos of Vladimir would see me from her place on my altar day after day at home and at Vespers on Saturday, complaining about being unlike anyone, being left out and alone. I'd complain that all the other stay-at-home moms I know hold things together: they make the dentist appointments, they clean the kitchen counter, they put away the laundry. All the other stay-at-home moms take a shower in the morning, they put on clean clothes, they brush their teeth. All the other stay-at-home moms go to the gym, revel in their children's scouting or sports or academic achievements. All the other stay-at-home moms are grateful they are at home; they want to be mothers, they want to be at home. We're not alike.

Mary, Queen of the Universe, would stare down at me from her perch high above, near the alcove, next to the altar. Her hands were held out from her sides, showing her clean, white skin, perfect nails, fingers soft and unscathed. Mary, Queen of the Universe, was never my role model when I was young; I prayed instead the prayers of St. Jude, patron saint of hopeless cases. I did not want to be a mother; I wanted to be a writer, I wanted to be an actor, I wanted to be a warrior and a poet and a singer and a songwriter. I wanted to be a punk rocker, foul-mouthed, notorious for sullen looks and moody lyrics. Mary, Queen of the Universe, had nothing to offer with her hands outstretched, so peaceful and serene, holding things together so perfectly, assumed bodily into heaven, intact, not left to decay here on Earth.

Surrounded by a deep gilded background, a sea of gold, the icon of the Theotokos of Vladimir often does not seem to see me there, standing near her during Vespers, in the quiet, in the dim light of Holy Trinity Orthodox Church. She looks beyond me, further ahead, past the place where I stand and into the pale future—hers, mine, ours. The cheek of the Christ child presses her face. He is in need. He is needy. His arm is wrapped around her neck, pulling her to him. "Look here," he says. I know those words; I know that hand on my neck, that cheek against my own.

When I make eye contact with her now that I, too, am a mother, I see something new in this woman. No longer Queen of the Universe and untouchable, I see her now, weary and fully woman—body aching, bone tired; even the Son of God has a child's needs and wants. Even the bearer of God's Son has a mother's needs and wants. She wants him to be healthy. She wants him to be happy. She wants him to get married, grow old and wise. Somehow in her heart she knows this will not happen. Somehow in her heart she knows that her fears for his future are both commonplace and cosmic.

When I go to her now, when I light the candle nearest her on my own icon stand at home and kiss her icon tenderly every morning, I am thinking about my children and about my fears—for them, for me, for us all. When I go to her now in the early morning hours, she sees me and we know each other. She gives me the "it's going to be all right" look I find myself giving to the harried mother in line at the grocery store, with children climbing on her back and her shopping cart, clinging and pressing their faces into her cheek. "Look, here. See me," they say. When I go to her now and kiss her icon tenderly every morning, I am thinking of that harried mother in line at the grocery store, and I am thinking of the woman who has never been that harried mother in the grocery store but always yearned to be, and I am thinking of the woman who has no need or desire to be that harried mother in the grocery store line, and I feel all of them in my skin, in my lips as I kiss the icon. We are, all of us, in this together, and Theotokos, God-bearer, touches my face and tells me in no uncertain terms that we are alike. We are all alike.

MY INNER PUNK ROCKER IS A FRAUD. MY inner punk rocker puts on a brave face, frozen sneer and eyebrow arched, but she is afraid too, afraid of being shunned, rejected, left out. She is willing to stare the lion down, not because she thinks she'll survive, but because she has no other choice, backed into the corner of the cage she built for herself. My inner punk rocker has kept me alive and protected even as she tips her hand time after time. She bristled at the suggestion that Orthodox women cannot accept communion when they are bleeding, the suggestion that a woman is unworthy, unclean, unwelcome merely based upon her God-made biology. So I calmed her down and dug for the reason behind the doctrine.

The roots of the practice begin long before the birth of Christ. It is Old Testament, it is Israelites wandering in the desert. The Hebrew word is *tuma*. English could not find a word for it, and so the word "unclean" became attached, but the essence of tuma is not dirt, shame, or filth. The essence of tuma is loss.

The Hebrews understood the body, the life, the essence of things in terms of loss and grief far better than most, and so tuma was the body of one who has died but also the body of the woman who has given birth. Where life had been, the essence of God resided; the space is holy ground, even after the life is gone. The body of one who has died has seen the essence of life escape it. The Holy exits this vessel. This is the loss.

The body of a woman who has given birth has seen the essence of life multiplied, grown, and departed from her. The Holy leaves a space in her not yet refilled. The woman who moves through the cycle of fertility, the possibility of new life creation that is unrealized, suffers that same loss. The potential of life is there; when that passes, this is the loss. For a time, she is repaired, she is renewed, she is filled again. She is too holy to touch because she is under reconstruction, readying for the potential of holy creation in herself once again.

In the Garden, I imagine the man lying there on the sand, staring at this new creature who is like him, who is nothing like him, this mysterious thing. Adam had no way to know that men would always find women as mysterious and magical as he found Eve. She, being creator as well, could make people of his modest offering. She, being mystical, was curious enough to ask about the forbidden fruit. She, being woman, was able to participate at a biological level in bringing God into flesh, the Word whispered into her body just like that first day of the world, the Word whispered into the darkness of her quiet womb; too holy to touch until that very moment, too holy to touch while she carried the Word, too holy to touch after He breathed the air outside her body for the first time. So then, Theotokos—God-bearer, Word-bringer, ordinary woman—she is all of us, speaks for all of us who are bleeding, all of us who have bled and waited and labored and grieved.

She knows, as my inner punk rocker knows, that I am always bleeding, I may always be bleeding in one way or another. She knows I am the woman on the road, reaching desperately for the robe of Christ. I can see Him turn at that touch, as if the healing energy began to unweave from his DNA, from His skin, from His robe the moment the thought came into my head and out from my lips, my arm outstretched: "I'm tired of bleeding." The healing was ready, I was ready, He was ready; too holy to touch. He found me there, along the road, and the road found me bleeding, and the road found me healing.

PART II

GIANTS IN THE ROAD

The idea of redemption is always good news, even if it means sacrifice or some difficult times.

—Patti Smith

Outside my apartment the street crews were tearing up the sidewalks. I sat on the skinny ledge of the modest bay window of my second floor walkup and smoked and watched them for a long time. I watched as they took jackhammers to the concrete. I watched as they moved past the rebar and into the long-hidden dirt down below.

This neighborhood was built up, literally, after the Chicago fire. What are now garden apartments were once street-level in many places. My second-floor walkup was a find, and the Polish landlord was patient with my late rent payments month after month, a side effect of being a recent college graduate working freelance in film production. The street crew made it impossible to write or read or watch television on the set my mother got for me after I left the live-in boyfriend that weekend only months before. I left the long-term relationship and the apartment I shared with my live-in boyfriend with my clothes, my car, and what was left of my self-esteem.

The street crew started early and knocked off at about the hottest part of the day, when it would be too hot for me to go and sit in the small side yard, so I sat in the window and watched them. I found as I watched them work that I wanted the large chunk of concrete with rebar sticking out the sides like metal rays of a grey stone sun. I wondered if it could be shaped and then displayed as some kind of urban sculpture. It was rugged, rough, and imposing. I thought it was beautiful. When I left my house that afternoon, the chunks of old cement sat patiently in a pile in the road, giants, waiting to be retrieved and taken away, and I had to change my normal walking route to the pub down the street to avoid them. The idea of it stuck with me for a long time, long after the concrete giants were gone, long after the crew was gone and the sidewalk reformed, drying while the neighborhood kids wrote their names in the still soft cement.

I am always only a few doubtful moments from running away.

The trip into Orthodoxy was not supposed to be a three-year plan, though most things I'd read about a typical catechumen's journey suggested one to three years of instruction and prayerful contemplation. I wanted to be fast-tracked. I don't like to wait. Each time I run across a giant in the road to becoming Orthodox, I wonder if it will finally be the deal-breaker. Is it strange enough, countercultural enough, hard enough to make me leave the dirt road and veer toward the superhighway running just over the next hill?

At each meaningful place along the road of Orthodoxy there was a detour, a side step or a delay, a giant in the road blocking my path. Walking into the door of an Orthodox Liturgy for the first time was a giant in the road. I moved slowly, making no noise, to get past him. I sat in the back, near the door. I spoke to no one. I made myself unavailable, invisible, stealthy. Once I was there and the territory began to look familiar again, I met a second giant—the guilt of leaving my family every week to begin a love affair with this faith without them. I was laying the groundwork, I was the scout sent ahead, like Jack planting beans and hoping for the best. No matter how victorious I felt when I had overcome an obstacle, there was always another giant waiting, looming ahead, making deep guttural sounds like thunder in the sky.

When I encounter those giants, sometimes I bob and weave, actively engaging them. Sometimes I taunt them, using all my reasoning, keeping my wits about me, and sometimes I make excuses and run away, or I hide in the bushes until they fall asleep and I creep by, their snoring ringing in my ears, reminding me of the danger that lurks in the dark, in the road, in the distance.

CHAPTER 9

FOLLOW

(on going it alone)

The beginning of love is the will to let those we love be
perfectly themselves, the resolution not to twist them to fit
our own image.

—Thomas Merton

The hardest part of the journey, harder than the struggles with prayer and fasting, harder than figuring out how to parent my crazy brood of chaos-makers during Liturgy, has been knowing that I was going first into this ancient tradition and that maybe my husband would never choose to become Orthodox at all. On some level I knew it was all right. My priest told me it was all right. I understood my relationship with God begins first in me; it has to begin in me. For as long as I seek to have my faith dependent on another person, it will always be shifting as that person shifts. No matter how strong and dependable he is (and he is strong and dependable), my husband will always be human, always changeable. Following God into Orthodoxy meant I was going it alone.

The whole idea of the man as spiritual head of the household had been brought up to me throughout the course of my conversion, albeit with a sideways sort of approach. It usually fell to about the third thing people would say about my decision to convert, after "Is it Jewish?" and "I've never heard of that." It's always a question, but I hear it as a judgment. I think I hear it as a judgment because I am, myself, judging. Moving into Orthodoxy was already a struggle, but to go it alone made it more awkward, the road more rock-filled, and no matter how often I heard from my priest that it would be all right in the long run, I still felt a certain loneliness when it came to this part. Every Sunday morning as I would push and shove the kids into clothing and shoes and coats, I would wonder if I was doing something ultimately harmful to my marriage by becoming Orthodox while my husband remained staunchly skeptical of organized religion as a whole.

I was not raised with the "head of the household" refrain in my ears. Twelve years of Catholic school and I can't recall ever hearing that phrase or concept. My introduction to this idea came through Dave and the Protestant circles he frequented. He was a former Nazarene, and when we met, he attended a popular, upbeat nondenominational church in Chicago.

I was suspicious. I thought he was too straitlaced for me. I'd never dated a "born-again Christian." Agnostics and Catholics were more my bag. I don't think it was a choice I made, to lean toward agnostics and Catholics, as much as those were the people I met, and it happened that for the most part even the agnostics I dated were former Catholics. We spoke the mother tongue together. It was dysfunctional even as it was comforting.

When Dave and I met, I wasn't going to church anywhere. I still considered myself a Christian mainly because I still fully believed the Creed. I had an understanding with God. I liked Him a whole lot. We talked every day, many times in fact. I believed in the reality of the Holy Spirit. I believed Jesus was who He said He was. I had no trouble with this. I had issues with churches.

I was on the outside and I kind of liked it that way. Moving away from home was exciting; moving away from my family faith was an adventure. I'd never really been to a Protestant church. It didn't even occur to me to try it. I guess I figured I'd just wander back into the Catholic Church when things lined up somehow. I was on a self-directed sabbatical from organized religion. I was the prodigal, but I always knew where I lived. I knew I could go home again when the time was right.

I was never the younger son in the story of the Prodigal. I had always been more like the older son who stayed home and did what he was meant to do. I would feel angry when Father Boyle would read the story to us in religion class, knowing full well I was missing the point he was trying to make, that God waits for us, that He sees us coming when we are still a long way off on the road. I was always more like the older son, responsible and angry, ready to rebel but too sensible to do it with anything more than passive-aggressive statements. For as rebellious as I felt as a teenager, I admit I was more afraid than adventurous. Each act of rebellion was measured and calculated. I did not jump off into the chasm but stayed on the spongy ground of the cliff above.

The difference between the Prodigal's family and mine is that the younger son left a home that stayed grounded and fertile. My home was transitional with my parents' divorce, torn up into pieces and glued back together on a regular basis. The glory of our family was that we found our way back to one another after each rip in the fabric of us. We were an emotional patchwork in progress, and I like to think I knew that somewhere deep inside. My teenage self was seething and angry, but she was protective and pragmatic enough to keep from adding to the frayed edges of our family struggle.

When our dating turned serious, Dave asked me point-blank what I believed where faith issues were concerned, and I told him. He asked what I thought about Jesus and I said, "Um . . . I like Him?"

He persisted, "Yeah, but do you think He was the Son of God?" and I said, laughing, because it was a ridiculous question to me, "Of course."

His last hesitation exposed his Nazarene roots a little. "What do you think about Mary?"

I thought about that for a moment. "I like her too."

"Yeah, but do you worship her?"

I'd had so little contact with the Protestant culture, I didn't realize this was a concern for anyone. The question was confusing. "Catholics don't worship Mary," I replied. All this served to ease his reservations about asking for my dainty hand in marriage, I guess, because not long after that he did propose to me in the back of a police car.

He'd borrowed my car that morning and picked me up later to have some lunch and retrieve his car from the shop. That he asked me to drive might have been a tipoff that something was up. He hated my driving, and I admit it's not without cause. I'm a terrible driver. But I followed his lead and took the wheel. He pointed the turn out to me almost too late, and I squealed my wheels to make the turn. The police car parked across the street pulled out from the curb and made the turn as well.

I had not had a ticket since I was 16, when I was caught doing 65 in a 35 zone, so the thought of breaking my law-abiding streak was unsettling. I turned down the alley to get to the parking lot of the taco joint and the police car turned too, his lights and siren kicking in, a voice on the speaker instructing me to pull over. I chose my spot, kept my hands on the wheel, and blamed Dave for it.

The policeman was a dark-haired, bulky South side cop,

and when I rolled down the window he asked for my license and registration in his thick Chicago accent. I handed it to him with shaking fingers, and he showed me his "hot sheet" for the day. My plate was listed there because, as he asserted, a car bearing that plate had been used in connection with a jewelry store robbery that morning. It did not occur to me that Dave had borrowed my car that morning, but he gave me a strange look when the policeman said it.

The cop had us step out of the car and told me he needed to search my car for evidence. I had watched too many episodes of *Cops* and I was beginning to growl about being unjustly accused. I insisted I was within my rights to watch him search the car and I edged out, leaving Dave with his hands placed flat on the hood of the car.

While the policeman rifled through the empty takeout containers and brown paper bags in my powder blue Hyundai, I watched and saw him slip something into one of them. He walked around to where I stood and pulled a heavy black revolver from the bag. He asked, "Is this yours?"

I panicked inside but said, almost calmly, "No, I saw you put that in there."

He reached into the bag again and pulled out a small velvet jewelry box, saying, "What about this?"

In my best indignant voice I responded, "I have never seen that before in my life."

He suggested we head downtown and I agreed, angry and defiant and ready to assert every known right I could pull from the long-gone days of playing the prosecuting attorney for the mock trial team in high school. He put me into the back of the squad car, and before Dave could follow I heard him say to the policeman, "Sir, I can explain."

They closed me into the back of the police car, and I watched as Dave waved his hands, trying to explain away what had become a very strange lunch date. After a few minutes, the policeman opened the door and Dave got in. He leaned forward, talking quickly. "Listen, I made a deal with the cop. You can either spend the rest of your life in jail," he said, pulling the box from his pocket, "or you can spend the rest of your life with me."

I gave the proposal a moment to sink in before I began to beat him about the head.

I got to know some of Dave's friends and began to visit his nondenominational church in Lincoln Park as I moved into the Protestant-church–visiting part of my religious journey. I never did find my groove there, though I did try. I wrote and performed songs a couple of times for the churches we attended. I joined the choir and the worship team at the Vineyard church. I wrote dramas for the nondenominational church. I helped with the children's ministry at the Presbyterian church.

No matter how I tried, there was always an empty piece for me. It was as though I was holding a space for that deep holy practice I used to know. I got affirmation of my creative work and acceptance from my peers; there were moments of connection at each of these churches, surely, yet there was something empty there, in me, some vitamin I was missing though I was barely aware of it. All I could do was to follow Dave and try my level best to be a part of it all without losing myself.

My greatest fear has always been that I might lose myself. I don't know if it stems from a deep wound at an early age or if I simply have this inborn desire to be special, to be set apart. Probably it is a combination of the two. In any case, it is a fear I have had to navigate with each life change I encounter. Entering high school, starting college, dating, moving to a new city, taking a new job, getting engaged, getting married, career choices, having children—all of these things lead me inevitably to the question, "Well, now who am I?"

My response in each of these situations was to try to be different—become a punk rocker instead of listening to Journey, be the only music composition major in the music program in college, date only outsiders and weirdos, move to Chicago with my band instead of finishing school in Ohio. Maybe even dating a Protestant was a mild rebellion against my Catholic upbringing. Despite my best efforts, I found I might have lost myself even so. Then when Dave moved away from organized religion just as I began to find my way home through Orthodoxy, the constant refrain piped up in me, "Well, now who am I?"

I'd like to say that I fully believe he'll end up Orthodox one day, but I can't say that. I just don't know, and I don't want it to matter. I worry more that I won't care, and that not caring means something dark and disconcerting about my heart, about our relationship. I want to care but I don't want to push. If there is anything I have gleaned on this long and dusty life road so far, it is that we are all moving at our own pace, that our traveling companions and our conversation partners merge or move on or fall back, that we recognize ourselves in the landmarks we pass and the company we keep. Sometimes we sit on the side of the road and wait for whatever comes next, sometimes we lead, sometimes we follow.

CHAPTER 10

INKED

(on tattoos and tantrums)

There is nothing so secular that it cannot be sacred, and
that is one of the deepest messages of the Incarnation.
—Madeleine L'Engle

The margins of my journals from high school were filled with doodles, chicken-scratch ideas for tattoos, and band names. The pages themselves housed song lyrics and wishes and dreams, rants, sighs, and homework reminders. It's painful to read them now. Clearly, being a teenager sucked.

With the benefit of years, I can see now why it was so hard to be a teenager. The modern American culture has a way of ushering us from childhood into a strange waiting area that includes an increase of responsibility but no increase in power. It's no wonder being a teenager was so gut-wrenching. In the pages of those journals, I see the progression of thoughts and feelings and attitudes ride the waves between the storm raging and the peaceful sea, when the whole world seemed far away, the horizon simply a line tracing the curve of the earth. In the margins of those pages I planned the person I wanted to be when I was finally on my own, with what I thought would be power and control added to my little boat on the big blue sea.

Before he proposed, Dave asked a lot of questions—some about faith, some about children, and a few about divorce. I'd never thought about it. The idea of divorce was a card in the relationship playing deck in my head. It was an option I kept open without ever really questioning it. When my parents divorced, it was still a stigma in our small Catholic community, but in the months before Dave proposed it had become a well-accepted practice when things didn't go well. The stigma faded over the short course of time between my parents' divorce and my adulthood. I allowed for the possibility of divorce in my own adult life, knowing what was at stake.

Before Dave proposed, he asked if I'd consider a "no-divorce" marriage, which sounded full-on crazy to me by then. The stinging reality of my previous engagement hit me in the gut before I answered, and I realized how I'd been holding that card in the deck for "just in case." Though it terrified me, I agreed to consider the no-divorce possibility, making stipulations for abuse and infidelity but not for much else.

My ability to surrender that card from the deck was so fluid, so smooth, that it surprised me, and it probably surprised Dave as well. The only explanation I can give is that releasing the divorce card, the "just in case" card, was a relief. Holding that so close to my heart for so long was exhausting. It made the prospect of marriage, with any guy, seem like a crap shoot, something a person would have to luck into, like the lottery. Giving the card up, setting it down on the table, meant that I was able to retake the responsibility for my own welfare. Marriage was not determined by the luck of the draw but by a recommitment every day to the person in front of me. Marriage, or at least my concept of marriage, changed in that moment. It became something new, something I'd never seen from inside, filled with possibility and struggle that leads forward instead of into retreat and abandonment. It intrigued me.

My family growing up was not simply uprooted in the divorce, it was perhaps never given the chance to really find its footing at all. The poorly rooted tree is still a tree, still needing soil, always looking for a lasting home to keep it upright in a storm. When the storm hit our family, our tree had no choice but to fall.

FATHER GREGORY WAS NOT SURPRISED BY my deal-breaker list. He'd seen lists like mine before. When we got to the question about my tattoos, he adopted his trademark shrug and a smile as he waxed rabbinical in his answer that I would not be obligated to have them removed. He warned about addiction, though, which I thought was a strange response. He said he knew people who could not stop once they'd started with tattooing and that it was a deeper problem, not the tattooing itself, but the filling of some unspoken need that only led to regret later.

My low blood pressure and measured bouts of needlephobia kept that from being a problem for me. I nearly fainted when the tattoo artist put the stencil transfer on me for my first tattoo. To go through that process meant a great deal of preparation and planning for me, finding the right artist, the right design, building up my confidence, eating enough to keep my blood sugar elevated and myself conscious.

It was the first meeting of the needle to skin that surprised me the most. It didn't pierce, like a blood draw or an injection; it was more of a scratching, a scraping along the first few layers of the epidermis. The first meeting of the needle to the skin is the outline; the needle moves quickly, sketching out the image. Over time, the vibration becomes relaxing and familiar. The sound of the needle is jarring, annoying, buzzing, intermittent with the lines that arc and bend; but it settles, eventually, into the background, blending with the traffic noise and casual conversation.

The first tattoo artist I hired was young, twenty-five at most, but the canvas of his skin was already covered with ink. He wanted to talk about Jesus because he was a Christian and he could tell from my design that I was also a Christian. He asked about the Celtic cross and about my faith. He railed about the organized church. He talked about grief and about abuse, and I listened. I tried to find common ground in his complaint, and in that moment I realized how old I felt. It was my fortieth birthday and this was my first tattoo, my midlife crisis tattoo. It had taken me this long to decide on a design and placement, to work up the courage to make the call, to work up the courage to have someone draw on my skin with a needle and ink.

My second tattoo was the Tree of Life, and it took shape on my left shoulder a few years later when I became a catechumen in the Eastern Orthodox Church. I had this notion of embracing the lost part of us, the part we were made for, the part we had turned away from in the Garden. I held to this idea that somehow representing this on my body would help remind me of the daily turning away from death, the daily turning toward the life offered. I wanted blue flowers for the Theotokos, the mother of God. I wanted the symbol of the Trinity woven into the leaves. I wanted it to be wild and beautiful, branches reaching. The artist this time was a woman I had met through a friend. Like the first artist, Serena, too, wore skin decorated with images, inks running into inks, on her hands, her feet, her neck. She had kind eyes, a gentle spirit, and skilled hands.

My first tattoo was hidden away, in a place even a bathing suit would cover easily. My second would show only if I let my arms and shoulders go bare, but my last tattoo resides on my left wrist. It was a butterfly originally meant to hover around the Tree of Life on my shoulder, representing beauty, truth, and goodness, representing rebirth and renewal. We had run out of time to add it on my shoulder, so when I returned to have the shading done on my tree, I decided instead to have the butterfly placed on my wrist. I imagined it would be small and inconspicuous, in a place where it would not stand out but where I could see it at any time. It brought to mind the ashes I wore each Lent on my forehead when I was a Catholic. But while the ashes of my youth reminded me of grief and longing, the tattoo here was meant to remind me of life and the start of new things, the promise of hope.

Serena scaled the butterfly up to a size she deemed appropriate for my tiny wrists and placed the stencil. It was larger than I'd expected. I stared at the stencil on my wrist a long time as she worked on adding some shading to the tree of life on my shoulder. She said she saw it in blue and I, too, saw it in blue, Mother Mary blue.

The tattoo on my wrist was far more painful than the other two since there was little between the skin and the sinew, tendons, and bones—the less padding offered, the more the nerves respond, messaging the brain that injury is happening. I breathed through the pain, ready to quit. I kept thinking it must be the halfway mark, but I had no way to know how far we were in the process. I could not stand to watch the tattoo needle greet my skin; I could only wait for the breaks Serena would take. I would grab a peek at the fresh, bleeding wound to gauge the time. When at last I'd think she was done, there would be more, so I'd grit my teeth, trying to make conversation to distract myself without taking her attention from her work. I breathed, reciting the Jesus Prayer through gritted teeth and spirit, letting the jarring sound and gripping pain of the needle do its work.

When I did see the progress, I was struck by how big the tattoo was, how bright, how blue. I worried that it was too big, too bright, too blue. I worried that I might regret this choice later, and I worried that it was too late. I was already too far committed on this road. The butterfly on my wrist, being sewn into my skin, echoed my fears about my journey into faith, into Orthodoxy: Was it also too big, too bright, too blue? Would I live to regret this after all the pain and struggle and planning?

"It's a little like getting married," I said, when asked about my conversion to Eastern Orthodoxy. People asked why it seemed to be taking so long, because it did seem to be taking a long time—at least three years from the start thus far. I thought to blame my shifting circumstances, my inability to remember key things about the tradition, the Liturgy, the fasting and prayer; but instead I simply said it was a little like getting married. I was headed to the altar, but there was still work to be done, caterers to book, invitations to pick out, premarital counseling to arrange.

Once I was chrismated, I intended Orthodoxy to be the last stop on my organized religion tour. I had already been Catholic and then had dated as many Protestant churches as I could while remaining intact. I kept feeling that if this Orthodoxy thing didn't work out, I was going to have to cloister myself where religion was concerned. I'd hide myself away, like Julian of Norwich, and wait for God's revelations sealed in an anchorite's cell. I'd write deep into the night in a kind of fever, scribbling down my inspired insights. I'd witness the action of the church through the window on one side of my cell—the chanting, the words, the incense. I'd witness the action of the world through the window on the other side—ready with a word of encouragement against the dirt and filth of life from my clean, protected cell, my self-imposed solitary confinement.

The skin's reaction to the needle and ink is to seal itself, to create a protective cover and scab itself over. After the pain and vibration of the needle comes the healing. The skin wants to heal; it wants to force out the ink and find itself again. The process of the tattoo is to guide the skin to heal while taking in the new information of the ink.

The method of healing varies from artist to artist, person to person. Serena instructed me to give the skin a short time to regroup after the initial event, then to offer it a kind of cauterization, sealing with hot water to rinse away the lotion, the dried blood, the remains of the stencil, the attempts to scar or scab. The skin wants to heal. If the artist goes too deep, too quickly, the ink is blurred, spreading out and destroying the image over time, fading into some unknown or unintended version of itself. If the artist does not go deep enough, the ink will fade and peel off in the healing process, leaving gaps in the image. Over the course of the weeks that follow, the skin will heal; it will take in the ink. The skin will make the ink a part of itself, healed softly with time and care.

Even now, a year later, the butterfly on my wrist catches

me by surprise each time I see it. I worry that perhaps it is too big, too bright, too blue; still, I know it is mine. It has grown into me as the Orthodox Liturgy has grown into me over time. When I am away from Liturgy for too long, I find I burn for it now, for the steadiness of the calendar, the words that ring out in repetition, the heavy scented air. When I return each week, I am coming home again. Liturgy is written into my flesh, sinking into my skin and my spirit.

The fear of regret is still present and may always be present: Is it too big, too bright, too blue? But the butterfly on my wrist reminds me of truth and beauty and goodness, the start of new things, the promise of hope. Like the tattoos I wear, this new journey is being knitted into my skin, healing softly with time and care, becoming part of me.

CHAPTER 11

LITTLE PROPHETS

(on bringing my kids to Liturgy)

*We spend the first twelve months of our children's lives
teaching them to walk and talk and the next twelve years
telling them to sit down and shut up.*

—Phyllis Diller

My youngest son, Miles, was the first to accompany me to the Orthodox Liturgy. I'd been making the long drive solo into Nashville to attend St. John's on Sunday mornings. There was no loss for anyone else in the household, seemingly. They slept in and ate pancakes when they woke.

I enticed Miles with the promise of pastries afterward, and he agreed. He sat on one of the benches against the wall, sighing heavily but not talking. It was a small room; he was intimidated, and I was distracted. A few times he asked how much longer, and I gave him an ever-decreasing number off the top of my head, completely inaccurate. I really didn't know what time it was. I was trying to be lost, out of time, in another zone, but Miles was ever present, and time feels different to a five-year-old with little experience in a church setting like this. He sighed, and then I sighed. He whispered, in his loud child whisper, "When it is over?" and I responded with a shaking of my head, with holding up five fingers, with tapping my wrist, a motion that means nothing to someone who doesn't wear a watch. Finally, I stood facing away from him, not asking anything of him as the Liturgy unfolded, simply letting him exhale loudly from his bench when he was so inclined.

The Presbyterian church in Nashville was still home to us for all intents and purposes. Our people were there even when our bodies stayed home and ate pancakes. Our people listened to me when I ranted about the state of the church in America. Our people nodded as I cried about my poor wandering spirit, about my husband's anger with religious authorities, about my children's lackluster participation. Our people took us out for drinks and invited us for barbecues and watched my children when we were in need. Our people loved us dearly and patiently, whether we showed up to the service or not, and that kept us afloat for a long time.

Here, standing in Liturgy, I was alone, apart from a couple of familiar faces. I always arrived late and left early, afraid of conversation, afraid of betraying our people at the Presbyterian church. Having Miles with me was a revelation of me, vulnerability, a peek into the wideness of my life. I don't know what I hoped for in that revelation apart from acceptance, assistance, the affirmation that I was not alone, that I was not set apart. At the same time, having my children around me in a new place, in a quiet place, gave me purpose, gave me context. Having Miles with me the first week showed my place in the world and gave me work to do when I was not sure what I was supposed to be saying, doing, or feeling in the long and confusing Liturgy. I got in touch with my own chaos-maker that first week. Rather than resent my son for his disruptions, I slid into my daily struggle of parenting, and that was far more familiar than the struggle to engage in Liturgy.

The first church we tried when we moved to Tennessee was huge, but we tried it anyway. Everything in my spirit rejected the megachurch model, but we were alone there in a new state, with four small children, homeschooling. I was desperate for connection with people, though I also feared it more than I could articulate. I wanted my children to make friends, to get some other voices in their lives than my husband's and mine, so we trotted the three oldest off to the "children's church" and moved into the sanctuary, me holding an infant Miles in my arms.

By the time the third usher at the megachurch tried to helpfully point me in the direction of the nursery for children under three years old, I was annoyed. I was ready to gently lay down the sleeping baby in my arms and offer the usher a greeting delivered by my clenched fist. I pondered this as he spoke, the smile never leaving his face. Rather than follow through on my knee-jerk, fist-punch response, I told him we were fine. He looked stunned and shrugged, as though no one had ever refused to put her child in the nursery before this. He pointed then to a darkened corner in the large auditorium. The cry room was surrounded by one-way glass. He let me know that it was soundproof and that the service was piped into the room via closed-circuit television. I could only manage a confused "wow" as I backed away to find my seat.

With each passing moment of the thirty-minute sermon I grew more agitated, crawling out of my skin and ready to roar like some alien creature I did not recognize. When the baby woke he did not cry, he cooed. I considered nursing him right there, in the middle of the crowded, non-kid-friendly auditorium, before God and everyone. I thought better of it and grudgingly moved toward the cry room, stomping and sneering all the way down the row. The room was dark and filled with weary parents. The children in the room were climbing on and crawling under the seats, the parents were chatting, the sermon was droning on, and I sat in the back row and nursed Miles while I cried, quietly drowned out by the rising worship music blaring from the speakers in the tiny room.

THE ORTHODOX PRIEST HAD DESCRIBED many times the short procedure that would take place before Liturgy the day the kids and I were received as catechumens in the Church. We would gather in the back, he would approach, and he would say a few prayers. At that point, he would ask if wanted to be received as catechumens, and we would answer, "We do." We would kiss his ring and he would pray again. It was simple. No matter how many times he described it to me, I could not keep the details in my head. I went over it with myself many times that week. I wanted to do it right; I was afraid of forgetting. I considered writing it on my hand.

Then, on the way to church that Palm Sunday morning, Henry announced he'd decided not to become a catechumen. At ten years old he was headstrong and intelligent. He asked to pray each night; he was eager to please; he had even expressed a desire to become an altar boy. His announcement was unexpected, but I let it go and agreed he was free to decide that. Moments later when we reached the church, he recanted the decision in favor of joining in again on the quest to become Orthodox.

I was already flustered by the time the ceremony began, and I realized too late that letting my boys take the palm fronds and pussy willows offered at the door was a really bad idea. They made the bunches into swords immediately, because their testosterone told them to, and then because they have no filter, they participated in swordplay the entire time we were being received. In retrospect, to everyone else it was probably not as bad as all that, but to me it was an unmitigated disaster. When it was over, I stewed about it in the back of the church, shooting angry glances at the boys every time they caught my eye, and feeling guilty about my anger at the same time.

THE ICON OF THE ARCHANGEL CAME FROM Pier One years before I ever considered becoming Orthodox. We bought it because it was beautiful. It was the last on the shelf. It was Raphael. While Gabriel brings messages and Michael brings swords, Raphael brings God's healing. I looked in vain for a long time for the other angels, stopping at Pier One stores whenever I saw them. Then later, when the Internet was in full swing, I searched, but I never found another like it. It was my first icon and the only one on my icon stand when I started attending St. John Chrysostom in Nashville.

By this time I was resolved to jump head-first into the practices, and so I took some votive candles and my prayer book, I stood Raphael up on the shelf at eye level, and I began to pray. It was not long before one or two children ran in to interrupt and not long past that they began to fight with one another on my bed. Then they rolled and wrestled on the floor, five feet from where I stood praying, then three feet from my prayers, then hands wrapped around my waist and my ankles begging for solutions to their civil wars, their boredom, their unceasing hunger.

I left off mid-prayer and growled without a trace of irony that I was praying and they should leave me alone. So they left the room while I swam in the regret of modeling this new practice really badly. I was not sure how I would find a way to integrate these new practices—the quiet, the prayer, the feasts and fasts, the ninety-minute Liturgy every Sunday—with the chaos-makers I parented every single day. It felt impossible. I lay on the bed face down for a moment, breathing into the pillow slowly and steadily, shaking my head from side to side with a kind of resigned moan.

Miles had entered the room again, quietly lying down next to me, and he slung his arm across my back, his small hand patting my shoulder. I turned on my side to face him, and he smiled as the others came into the room one by one, crawled softly onto the bed, and snuggled in, until finally we were all there in the embrace of arms and legs, anger drained away as the chaos-makers became little prophets. They told me it was all right, we were all right, it was going to be all right, and I chose to believe that.

When we all are very old, I imagine my children will remember most how consistent I was in my inconsistency. I imagine they'll tell people about how cranky I was while I was writing but how happy and loving I was when I finished for the day. I imagine they'll mention the trial and error with their home-school curriculum and scheduling but also my commitment to their creative and emotional growth. I imagine they'll tell stories about my bouts with veganism and then all-meat diets, then juicing, then green-smoothie diets. They'll remember that I was a virtual Jekyll-and-Hyde of eating plans, but also that I instructed them to love the bodies they were given, to fuel them well.

In the end, when I am very old, I hope they will also tell about those early years of my conversion when I was confused and frustrated and often angry but kept on even so. I hope it will be a redeeming story of the pursuit of something beautiful and good; that we will laugh about my wanting to swear whenever I stood at the icon stand in those first years as I fought to reach around or float above the chaos instead of swimming in it. I hope that whether they choose to become or remain Orthodox when they build their own lives and their own brand of chaos, they will remember something good and true and pure about those days when I was fighting the sandstorm, when I was taming the wind. I hope they will know in all of it that quiet needs cultivating, watering, nurturing, and time. I hope they will see that I was cultivating the quiet on that long and dusty road.

CHAPTER 12

REFORMATION

(on conversion)

*People can change anything they want to. And that means
everything in the world. People are running about following
their little tracks—I am one of them. But we've all got to
stop just following our own little mouse trail. People can do
anything—this is something that I'm beginning to learn.*
　　　　　　　　　　　　　　　　　　　　—Joe Strummer

*The more I considered Christianity, the more I found that
while it had established a rule and order, the chief aim of
that order was to give room for good things to run wild.*
　　　　　　　　　　　　　　　　　　　　—G.K. Chesterton

S he needs the structure," my friend Beth told me that day
over lunch. "She's so crazy and creative," she said of her
preteen daughter, "that it helps her to know she has a

safe school setting. She knows where the boundaries are." Her daughter was beginning Catholic school for the first time as a preteen. She was excited for the structure, for the oversight, for the school uniform.

I thought of myself at that age, ironing my Catholic school uniform and doing a poor job of it. Apart from the ironing, I didn't mind wearing a school uniform. I wore a uniform of one plaid or another for twelve years: eight years of grade school at St. Teresa and four years of high school at Mother Seton. Having a uniform made it easier for me to know how I was different from everyone else. It was easier to rebel against a uniform; when everyone is an individual there's really nothing to rail against.

The kids at St. Teresa of Avila still wear the same plaid of the uniforms I wore as an eleven-year-old, but the girls' skirts have box pleats now, with wide, deep-creased lines folding in at the front, sides, and back of the skirt. Our uniform skirts in 1978 had knife pleats circling the entire skirt in one-inch accordion-like bands from waist to hem. After washing, they looked like rolls of fat fabric fingers. My job once a week, when I had reached a certain age, was to restore the crisp lines with the steam iron.

There was no way to cheat at it; there was no quitting halfway through. To shirk the ironing of the pleats would be an advertisement of sloth and neglect on my part. It's no accident that I don't iron anything at all now. That uniform skirt was the only piece of clothing I was ever required to iron, and to this day I go out of my way to buy clothing that won't tie me to that task again. And while I don't miss ironing duty, I can appreciate the Zen-like practice of it, and I wonder where that shows up in my life now. I wonder then if this pursuit of Orthodoxy with its fasting and prayer and Liturgy is a way of returning the crisp edges to my self, to my faith. There was something holy in those lines I would restore every week in that uniform skirt, something calming for that young girl. There was something holy in those boundaries, something safe and secure. It's not until just now, as I begin to embrace Orthodoxy, that I realize how much I need to know where the boundaries are; I need to begin to restore the crisp lines in the fabric of me.

I'D NEVER HEARD OF REFORMATION SUNDAY, probably because I was raised Catholic. My knowledge of most things Protestant was lacking at best. The cover of the program for church showed praying hands and proclaimed the day as "Reformation Sunday." I listened as the pastor spoke on the importance of the date, even tearing up as he preached the value of the day to Christians.

Inside, I was already absent. I had left his sermon and this church long ago. Each time someone I knew changed churches, and each time I heard the four-point sermons, and each time I looked out the window and wished I were in bed, I left the church a little bit more. By the time I began to explore becoming Orthodox, I was already halfway out the door, reaching in now and then to keep my children in some kind of "program" of faith, reaching my hands forward to the friends who still showed up week after week. These were my people, and I loved them. To leave felt like a betrayal, an abandonment of this last vestige of church life.

As I listened to the pastor talk, I came to the stunning realization that I'd never been a Protestant. Since wandering away from Catholicism, I had never joined another church, never made a profession of a new faith. I clung to my Catholic roots with everything I had. I defended them to anyone who would attack the church of my family and my friends and my youth. In many ways, I'd always been Catholic, and I always would remain, at a basic level, Catholic.

Father Gregory met with me in the temporary space they'd given him to use as an office while Holy Trinity was undergoing its renovation. The office was cramped, crowded with boxes of books and pamphlets and paperwork. His computer sat on a small wooden desk barely big enough for the mouse to move on its pad. He was looking up a book title he'd suggested to me as I told him about Reformation Sunday. As he clicked, I wondered aloud about never being a Protestant, and it occurred to me that maybe now, in becoming Orthodox, I was in some sort of protest against the norm. "Because of the schism," I pondered. "Would that make the Catholics or the Orthodox the Protestants? Who was the protester?" He looked up from his computer, confused, unable to find the right language to answer the question. He laughed a little, assuming the question was probably more rhetorical than not.

MY SENIOR YEAR AT SETON HIGH SCHOOL,
I drew anarchy symbols and wrote lyrics to punk songs in the
light gray-and-white boxes on my uniform skirt. I hemmed the
skirt higher than knee level but not high enough to be placed
into the "slutty" category. By the end of that year, I had quietly
frayed the edges of that skirt, I wore my white shirt untucked,
left the historically crisp edges of the pleats open to curve the
way the fabric wanted to go. I let my hair go strange and my
attitude expand, because freedom was coming, this era was end-
ing, college was ahead, and everything was new and ready and
possible.

College was a chance for me to be re-formed, to become
the version of myself I was never able to be in high school or
in my small parish of St. Teresa of Avila, where everyone knew
me. Every new branding of myself during those teenage years
was tempered by the history there, by the family secrets handed
out at the passing of the peace and the unspoken lore of what
good Catholic girls were supposed to do and not do. At college,
away from home for the first time ever, I could be mysterious,
outrageous, quiet, and defiant. I could be anyone I wanted to
be. It was exciting and unsettling to take the reins of my life in
college, knowing I was no longer obligated to fit myself into the
mold everyone else seemed content to press into.

Beth had tried homeschooling with Grace. Her artist-mom
temperament made her a natural life teacher, and Grace's sweet
and low-key attitude was an art of its own. It sounded good
on paper, this pairing of freedom and bonding and making the

world a vast learning environment. The combination turned out to be chaos, but not the kind she'd seen at my house day after day. Ours was testosterone-fueled and experiment-driven. We tried a new curriculum whenever we were bored, which was often. We tried outside school. We tried co-ops. It probably looked free-form and spirited to most people on the outside. It probably looked appealing.

The reality was that after years of homeschooling, I was lonely for adult company, I was desperate to do the homeschooling thing well, and I was sorely afraid of the outside world. I'd folded in on myself. What had begun as a beautiful time of connection with my kids was slowly turning to resentment on my part. When Beth told me about the new plan to send Grace to school after their brief bout of homeschooling, the first thing she said was that Grace needed structure. They both needed it. A twinge of loneliness hit me hard, and I knew she had it right. They needed structure because it allowed them both to be wild in their art lives. It allowed their minds to be elastic and supple. It allowed them to become who they were meant to be.

So Grace donned the plaid uniform that looked so familiar to me from my own Catholic school days, and it stirred in me all kinds of memories and a little bit of jealousy, too. I needed structure. I didn't want to always be the schoolteacher. I didn't want to have to have all the answers and be the quiet, steadfast one all the time. Not only did I not want to do it, I felt I was failing when I tried. We struggled through another few years of homeschooling, trying new curriculums and outside tutorials to get me through.

My daughter began her foray into "real school" finally as a sophomore after our move back to Chicago. All of my worst high school memories came from my freshman and sophomore years, but I tried to set those aside as I shopped for her school supplies. I set them aside as we spoke about what to expect, and I set them aside when I dropped her at the front door of the building because she did not want or need me to walk her in. She waved to me as I sat in the car, and when she was gone, I drove a few blocks and pulled over to cry.

When Dave complains about the unchanging nature of the Orthodox Church, I let him complain. It's possible he doesn't need the structure, he doesn't need the rule and the order for his "good things to run wild," as G. K. Chesterton would say, but I know that I do. I need that rule and order so that I can find my own re-formation of faith.

We spent a great deal of our marriage working at church plants or rebrandings or re-formings of dying churches. When we first considered moving back to Chicago from Tennessee, Dave met with our old friend and former leader of Metanoia, now leading a vibrant reboot of a church in the suburbs of Chicago. It was a good meeting; they spent time reconnecting, they fell back into their friendly, familial arguing about the nature of God, and they made some headway in their differences. Life on the Vine was beginning to plant some new churches at that time, and hidden in the conversation we had about it was an unasked question that hung there between us. It was the question we would always ask when presented with some new adventure or opportunity: "Should we?"

I let the question hang there, drifting around the room, while I checked in on myself and wondered if this might be the re-forming of us once again, and I wondered if this might be the re-forming of Dave in his journey of faith. I let the question hang there unasked, unaddressed, until finally I said I would support whatever he embarked upon in Chicago, but I was going to become Orthodox. I said I would join in with any events, I would walk alongside, I would be a part of it as much as he needed, but I was becoming Orthodox.

My greatest unspoken fear in going it alone into Orthodoxy was that one day Dave might find his way into some kind of organized faith, that he might be re-forming himself and wondering what that might mean to me, to us as a couple and to us as a family. I spoke that fear, and I let that take up the space around us for a little while. It was two years before we finally made that move to Chicago. Dave slipped further from organized religion while I moved steadily, with intention and with apprehension, into the comforting rule and order of Orthodoxy.

CHAPTER 13

A SINNER

(on prayer and profanity)

*Pray simply. Do not expect to find in your heart any
remarkable gift of prayer. Consider yourself unworthy of
it—then you will find peace. Use the empty, cold dryness
of your prayer as food for your humility. Repeat constantly: "I am not worthy, Lord, I am not worthy!" But
say it calmly, without agitation. This humble prayer will
be acceptable to God.*

—Elder Macarius of Optina

*Basically, I'm for anything that gets you through the
night—be it prayer, tranquilizers, or a bottle of Jack
Daniels.*

—Frank Sinatra

Sometimes I want to start cussing as I begin to think about becoming Orthodox. When I think about praying or about fasting, I want to swear profusely. I know what it is, this propensity to break into expletives. I know it's that lasting vestige of punk rocker living deep inside of me, clinging to that tattered T-shirt and army surplus jacket I keep hidden away. I know it is that teenage part of myself giving the middle finger to the authority figures I've so carefully chosen to guide me in this next part of my spiritual life. After this long struggle to be a part of some ancient faith tradition without losing myself in the process, I move toward this highly structured and seemingly old-fashioned way of belief. Of course my rebel psyche is clawing its own eyes out—how could I expect anything else?

It all comes of a dirty nous. The Greeks used the word *nous* to describe that part of us that defies description. It is not the intellect, nor is it the soul. When I think of the nous, I always picture a lens of sorts, as in "seeing through the glass darkly," amplifying or clouding my view. I see the windows in my Chicago apartment that face the busy street outside. All day and all night the street gives easy access to cars, trucks, and motorcycles spewing black smoke, polluting the already weary Chicago air, and the evidence of it shows up on these windows. The mechanical world must hate clean windows. The windows are assaulted inside and out, day after day after day. I could clean them, with enough vinegar and water, rags and newspaper, but I don't do it. It falls to the bottom of my list every single time. Prayer is this.

Prayer is the window cleaning. It comes as no surprise, then, this polluted lens of mine, this dirty nous.

The small pocket prayer book arrived in the mail only a few days after I arrived home from a retreat. I was just putting my feet on the ancient road, making plans to visit churches, writing emails to priests. The prayer book contained the most common Orthodox daily prayers and the whole of Sunday Liturgy between its thin covers. I sat on my bed that first day and read through the prayers, recognizing only a few phrases here and there. The mealtime prayer was similar to the one we used growing up, but the nighttime prayer was foreign. There were prayers for morning, afternoon, evening, sickness, children, spouses, military, confession, feast days, and fasting.

I had become so used to my off-the-cuff, chatty and conversational praying style that conforming to the written prayers was a stretch. I bristled at the thought of it, picking up the book and setting it down throughout the day. It was like swimming with my clothes on when I tried to recite the formal, stuffy prayers, and I resisted it each time. I hoped it would not always be like this, feeling that a prayer life was putting on cement shoes and a three-piece suit before jumping into the river. I saw myself spinning out again and again with the struggle. I tried to picture that each line of recited prayer I offered throughout the day was water dripping down the mountainside, wearing away the rocky exterior, prayer becoming word becoming flesh, becoming profanity, becoming profundity. Prayer needed practice, and I carried the prayer book with me in my purse so I could work that practice discreetly into daily life—praying morning, afternoon, and evening as often as I remembered.

In the morning, I feel so optimistic. It's as though early morning was made for prayer. Everything is tender at the start; everything is possible, plausible, palpable. The icons wait for me, raising an eyebrow as I pass them on the way to the coffeepot. Caffeine-fueled, I address them finally and light candles for my day, for my friends' day, for my children, for my fear, for my doubt. I need more candles. I need a lot more candles. I used to hide when I did this, afraid my children would think I was weird, afraid my non-converting husband would think I was putting some pressure on him. I question my own motives, feeling stiff and tired and awkward, but I gave up this questioning of motives for Lent one year. Now I light candles and try to pray no matter who is up.

Then I call the middle of the day "three o'clock crazy." In the middle of the day, no matter how I might seek out time to be alone and pray, my calendar is wildly uncooperative here. I find that though I might crave the possibility afternoon prayer promises, and though it all seems clear and right, I just can't muster it. I try to remind myself it's good for me, that it is hydration rather than duty. My soul is dried out and wilting, and although I know I ought to be downing those many ounces of water, I fail. I always fail. It's the workout I considered and rejected at every turn with "maybe later." I don't make time. I don't think about it for hours at a time, it seems. And then the three o'clock crazy hits, and the day has gotten away from me, and there is housework and schoolwork and dinnertime prep and thinking about tomorrow or the next day. By three o'clock, my day is gone, and in its place is regret and resentment. There is no room for prayer. The tension builds, and I have no reserves. I go Mount Vesuvius on my family. I begin to think I am on my own, there is no help in sight, and the future of the whole world rests with me. Then when I consider prayer, I just want to pull on my combat boots and start cussing again.

When evening comes and I'm exhausted after getting the kids in bed, I am tortured with doubt and fear. The day has fallen into me; everything I left undone develops a voice and starts to nag. Everything I thought I relied upon begins to kick me under the table, and I find I no longer remember why I ever began the process of becoming Orthodox. The elements of the practice—Liturgy, prayer, fasting—these are a pain, not worth the effort. At night, when I am trying my best to get to sleep, I am wide awake and worried. At night, when I am trying to get to sleep, I don't want to be Orthodox. I just want to rest. I want life to be easier. I want the voices of doubt and fear to leave me alone and go bother someone else for a little while.

Sometimes, late at night when the house is quiet, I can write. Not always and not often. Every once in a while, when it's late at night and the house is quiet, I can write, and the writing is a kind of prayer. I suppose I always thought it was the words I put down on the paper or the effort it took to wait for the quiet and to keep myself conscious; but I know now it isn't what I write or perhaps even the act of writing. Now I know that it's prayer, because it makes room for something holy to happen. I'm clearing away space and letting it get filled up with whatever I've been holding at arm's length all day.

"Maybe later" repeats over and over, and the pile on my desk gets no smaller. Simple things like signing my sons up for sports or Boy Scouts, paying the water bill, or wiping down the kitchen counter are monstrous, because the catalogue of things I haven't done but have yet to do comes crashing down on my guilty head. Of course there is no room for the quiet. Of course I'd rather cuss than pray. Of course I'll have to get to prayer later.

It's later. And so I sit down and I let it be later, and I let the words come, and I let the silence sit next to me, take up residence in me, and as I listen to the clicking of my keyboard, I am not worried. I am not concerned about the laundry list languishing on top of the refrigerator. There is only now, only this quiet, this moment, these words, this sort of prayer. I write about praying without ceasing, and I launch into some strange grief about why I can't make housework into prayer. I wonder why, amid all my talk of finding God in the quotidian, I can't seem to channel the calm advice of Kathleen Norris no matter how hard I work at it. I chide myself that I won't even draw one moment during the day to recognize the holy when it's dressed in the same shirt it has been wearing for weeks. I see the holy, and all I can think is, "Oh, God, I have to wash that damn shirt."

In the night, I can feel the deep crease in my brow furrowing into a Grand Canyon. I don't know what to make of my doubt and my fear. I find myself crying out and asking God to save me from this moment of faithlessness. I ask Him leading questions like, "This is really stupid, isn't it?" and "You would tell me if this was a gigantic mistake, wouldn't you?" followed by, "Who is going to save me from myself?"

To these questions, I suppose what I want is some kind of comfort, some kind of heavenly choir singing to soothe my weariness. In that moment I open my heart to welcome this kind of response, and I am greeted only with silence. My inner therapist tells me that this makes sense. I am working muscles I have not exercised before. There will be some discomfort, some pain. I just have to keep at it. My inner therapist tells me to chill out, get a grip, and take a Xanax, but I don't have any Xanax.

Father Gregory let me take one of the red-covered books of the Divine Liturgy from the church after Vespers one night. I wanted to learn Greek, to be able to say the words with some understanding and follow along easily, without stumbling. I practiced them at home, but I was only ever able to remember the repetitive refrains of *Kyrie* when the time came. I had to keep my face glued to the book, and that felt like a loss.

I had not met anyone at the church; I was alone, still absent my family. I wanted to learn Greek, to be able to enter in on a deeper level, so in addition to the Liturgy book, I found a program for my phone and my computer that promised to teach Greek, but it became clear they were made more for tourists. Apart from learning how to say "yes" and "no" along with the phrases, "I am a dolphin trainer" and "You are a very good dancer," I did not gain much there.

In the end, the only Greek I was able to master on my own was the Jesus Prayer. It was the one Orthodox prayer in English that issued from me easily when all other words failed; perhaps that is why it stuck to me so easily in Greek. I listened to the words recorded slowly. I noted where I ought to place the emphasis, the curving of the tongue over the "r" of the Kyrie, letting the last sounds of each word fall off casually—*Kyrie Iesou Christe*. I rolled the words around in my head as I drove, as I showered, as I made beds and did laundry and washed dishes, until I had them embedded somehow in my skin, until they came without thinking in the most ordinary moments, sometimes strung together, sometimes in pieces.

One night while my son was praying softly in his bed, I heard him say in that loud kid-style whisper, "Please, God, do not let anything bad ever happen to us."

I had just told them about the fire ladder in their closet. One night, in a bout of fear-fueled insomnia, I had ordered the fire ladders for the children's rooms. I had been imagining the scenarios, the "what would happen ifs," and each time I fell deeper into fear. The potential loss was so close to me I could feel the tears on my face from the manufactured memory. I walked from room to room a number of times in the dead of night until I finally sat down at the computer and ordered fire ladders. It was all I could do, and it got me to sleep that night.

When I placed the heavy folded ladder in their closet, they gathered around, excited to find out about the latest add. I explained in my calmest, most matter-of-fact voice its use. I aimed my comments at Chet because he was the oldest, telling him he needed to access this in case of a fire. I saw on their faces in that moment that the idea of a fire had never occurred to them. They took in the information, asked a lot of questions, and I watched as they sopped up the possibilities like a sponge, adding this new language of fear to their untroubled day.

Twelve-year-old Chet was praying then, softly, that nothing bad would ever happen to us, and I silently questioned my methods, my toxic sharing of my own fears. But it's better to be prepared, I thought. I sat on the edge of his bed and I put my hands on his face, kissing his forehead, instructing him about prayer and protection and language. I instructed him to pray for peace and for strength and for presence of mind in troubled times, because apart from buying fire ladders, it is all we can do. I try to be convincing even as so often I am unconvinced in those moments.

Sometimes, late at night when the house is quiet, when I am worried and I cannot sleep, when I am restless and afraid, and there is nothing I can do, nothing I can buy, no ladder I can build to protect myself, when I have nothing else to medicate me, I try to lay aside the anxiety in favor of the Jesus Prayer. At first, I struggle, like wading through mud, and it feels as though I am merely trying to talk over those fearful voices in my head because, in fact, I am. Though I fall into the Jesus Prayer easily because of its rhythm, its predictability, its certainty, it is also maddening at first. I find myself pounding the words like nails into a board:

Lord JESUS Christ

Son OF GOD

Have MERCY on ME

A Sinner.

LORD

JESUS

CHRIST

And each word is punctuation and each word exasperation and each word wonder and awe and readiness and willingness and hope and hell and fury. Then I realize, quite strangely, with time and persistence, my prayer becomes quiet and slow, deep and powerful. I find I am no longer even thinking the words or saying them aloud. It is as if they exist apart from me, apart from my doubt and worry. Each word, each syllable is a soft-treading footstep, propelling me forward, somewhere unknown or somewhere known but forgotten. At my feet the road is no longer mud but stone, cold and sturdy, clear.

And the quiet tells me something then—it whispers urgently in my ear, runs its fingers through my hair. The quiet tells me it is always present and always present-tense. It tells me prayer doesn't need to wait for the quiet to come, but the quiet waits for the prayer even so. It waits for the late-night clicking of fingers on the keyboard, for the steady breathing, for the words that have been circulating in an overworked mind, an exhausted body, in a fearful heart. The quiet waits so beautifully, so eternally, so patiently for the prayer. The quiet is so thankful for the attention when it comes and is never angry when I'd rather go to sleep than keep it company.

But sometimes, late at night, the words are only whispers—
Lord Jesus Christ, Son of God. The quiet is kindness and gratitude and calm—Have mercy on me, a sinner. And I fall asleep
like that, the words of the Jesus Prayer melting from English
to Greek—*Kyrie Iesou Christe*. Floating around me—*Yie tou
Theou*. Swimming apart from me—*Eleison me*. The words
becoming water, *tin amartalon*. Repeating and repeating and
repeating, the last thing I remember:

Kyrie Iesou Christe

Kyrie Iesou Christe

Kyrie Iesou Christe

Kyrie

Kyrie

Kyrie

CHAPTER 14

No Room

(on being too busy to be Orthodox)

The busy have no time for tears.

—Lord Byron

You who fasted and you who have not fasted, rejoice together. The table is fully laden: let all enjoy it.
——The Paschal Homily of St. John Chrysostom

I was too busy to leave my family to go to Garnet's funeral. She was a second mother to me growing up. Her daughter Margaret was my age, my best friend since kindergarten. They lived behind us when we lived on Loretta Avenue. Our backyards stretched out like limbs of two trees touching, the way our bare feet touched when Margaret and I sat on the hot sidewalk together in the summer, talking about the Monkees, *Gilligan's Island*, her older sister's boyfriends. I thought when I met her that Garnet was Margaret's grandmother. She was far older than my own mother. She had given birth to eight other children before Margaret came along. Margaret was the classic Catholic change-of-life baby.

Garnet was an old-school German housewife, mother, and grandmother, stern when she wanted to be and sweet just as easily. She cared deeply about her family, and she adopted me into that family, calling me daughter number seven and expecting me to do my fair share of the chores on Saturday mornings when I would show up at their door. She would scrub her floors every day, whether they needed scrubbing or not. Her knees were calloused and darkened under the hem of her housecoat, her arms strong and ready for an embrace.

But I was too busy to leave my little family to go to Garnet's funeral when she died, years after I left Ohio. The drive from Nashville to Cincinnati seemed impossible with small kids at home and my husband away in Chicago on business. I wrestled with the decision for days, changing my mind back and forth, strategizing and planning and scrapping it and then crying because I felt I ought to be there, daughter number seven, away without leave.

But it had been years since I'd seen her. The last time, she had been in the back bedroom on the first floor of Margaret's house. She'd moved in with them in the last years of her life. Garnet sat in a rocking chair reading a small Catholic prayer book when I entered. She could hear next to nothing, found little to keep herself occupied, and Margaret said she was irritable, but she recognized me right away and moved to stand. I waved for her to stay seated, knowing moving was hard for her, but she stood anyway, the prayer book falling from her lap as she hugged me. I picked up the book as she told me I was still too skinny. As I handed the book back to her, I saw how tattered it was, the edges worn, the cover ripped. Notes were scrawled in the edges, names of children and friends and relatives were written on a blank page at the back. She shrugged when I suggested she get a new copy of the book. "It's old, like me," she said and smiled a little.

Margaret understood about my decision to stay home from the funeral. If she was disappointed, she never let on. I was disappointed, though, feeling that grief come over me while I put the kids to bed or while I washed my own kitchen floor days later. The grief was the loss of the woman I called my second mother, but more so, it was that I felt I was too busy to break away and say goodbye to her. Regret made the loss palpable. My Catholic guilt about never being good enough or thoughtful enough or wise enough rose up in me like an old, unwelcome friend. Even now, I wish I had made time for it.

There is no room in my life for Orthodoxy. My life is simply not organized in such a way as to really allow me to engage this practice—to make time to pray, to find a community, to commit to new people, even to attend Liturgy. I just don't have the room for it. I don't have the space for it, and this is the reality of my situation.

It's distressing, but this is no surprise. I knew that to be a part of this tradition meant a degree of sacrifice. I knew it meant making time for Liturgy, making room for prayer and fasting, making new friends. I knew that, and I had a timetable in my head around when I'd be able to fully execute all these elements into a well-oiled and solid-state machine of religious practice. I imagined I'd be all in, so to speak, by September of that first year as a catechumen.

I toyed with the idea of just jumping in, persuading someone to back me up so I could just get my badge and become a card-carrying member of the Eastern Orthodox Church. I'm not usually a joiner, but I wanted desperately to be "in," as if that would make the practices easier somehow. Time itself was a giant in the road, blocking my way, making noises like a ticking bomb.

What stopped me from being able to fully get into the groove of Orthodoxy always seemed to be external. If I lived alone, if my circumstances were different, if it were just me, this would all be a cakewalk. But in real life, I'm not alone, my circumstances are what they are, and it isn't just me. I'm a functioning member of a group of chaos-seekers. I'm a fully sanctioned partner in a marriage. I need to pay attention to these parts; these relationships are primary and immediate, and this isn't bad or wrong; it's merely incomplete, at best. My family is changing always, developing, in crisis, in joy, in motion all the time. We change schools, we change diets, we change churches, we change cities, and the question that always crops up no matter what the change is, "Where are we anchored now?"

When I was a kid, I was anchored in the Catholic Church because it was the mooring place of my family. Even when I wandered away from my Catholic practice, I still had that anchoring. I was reminded of that by the prayer cards I kept in my jewelry box, the conversations I had with God out loud in my car, the twinge I felt whenever I passed a Catholic church on Sunday mornings while the bells rang, calling to me as I sped up toward the $5.99 pancake breakfast at the Waffle House down the road.

I have lived without any other kind of anchoring a long time now in so many areas of life. That most basic level of religious faith, that Catholic part, is the one constant throughout all the transitions I encountered—in dating, schooling, housing, partnering. Despite my turning away and my rebellion and my searching, I know the sweetness of faith as well as the bitter taste of fear, the memory of each lingering. I was anchored in the Catholic Church, and when I wandered away I dragged that anchor across the ocean because it felt safe and secure. Pulling up that anchor now and feeling the movement on the open sea as I move toward becoming Orthodox is overwhelming. Taking up new practices is overwhelming, and so I revert to old habits, to being too busy, to making excuses. It's too much. It's too demanding. I don't have time for this. It shouldn't be this hard.

I'll admit I'd prefer to find religious practice I can purchase online so that I can have it delivered to my door. I'd like to be excited to find it on the porch when I get home one evening, take my time opening it and unpacking it all, marveling at all the intricate, delicate moving parts and wondering aloud at the craftsmanship. This life would look super on my mantle just above the fireplace. I would dust it faithfully so that it never tarnished, so that it was always ready for viewing by visitors. This is the part where I'm supposed to make some realization that this is not at all the life I'm after, that to wait and chip away at the obstacles and challenges is going to culminate in the authentic expression of faith. I do want that, that is the goal here, but I won't lie: that online option looks mighty good. It would be quite the time-saver.

This present moment is sometimes inconvenient. It was late. The boys were supposed to be in bed already long ago, but bedtime has always been a constant struggle in our house. No matter what the child-rearing books suggested, we just could never wrestle the boys into any kind of a regular and lasting routine. Every bedtime found me cranky and prone to angry outbursts and martyr-like rants.

With our firstborn, we cultivated lovely moments before bed, we delighted in every coo, and we watched her fall asleep on our laps while we sighed with joy. We had the luxury then of allowing for the moments, making space for those tender things we'd want to have emblazoned in our memories. With our firstborn, we had the benefit of time and energy and working from home. With the three boys that followed, we had years of sleep deprivation under our belts, we had an expanding brood and an expanding business, and moving from one state to another and homeschooling and pounding cups of coffee to keep it all together. For a length of time, every task was an uphill climb, and bedtime was to be feared by the parents and avoided by the children.

One night, it was late and the boys were running, dancing, fighting, fueled with some unseen energy force that made the room vibrate while their voices clashed. Miles came into our room because I had given up. I was lying in my bed, pretending to read a book, and I begged Dave to get the boys in order, to get Miles back to his room and his bed. Then Miles began to sing a road trip song. I thought I might lose my mind as those ants went marching two by two, hurrah, hurrah, but Dave joined in, fully present, fully willing and able.

I watched them there, singing, dancing, trying to remember the words for each number, and it slowly wore down my cranky exterior. By the time they reached six by six and were missing the words, I chimed in "pick up sticks!" without even thinking, and I shocked myself at how beautiful this moment had become—my daughter reading quietly in her room, my older sons laughing and yelling in their room, and my husband and my youngest boy singing about ants marching. It was a holy moment, and we made room for it. It was late and there were things to do the next day, responsibilities and commitments, but we made room for the chaos and the beauty and the ants marching six by six, hurrah, hurrah.

THE CANON OF ST. ANDREW INVOLVES A lot of prostration, which is falling to the knees, hands and forehead touching the ground, holding there a brief moment, and then bringing the body back to standing. The Canon of St. Andrew involves this act punctuating most, if not all, of the troparia, which are short hymns or stanzas. The refrain that accompanies the prostrations echoes through the congregation after each troparion: "Have mercy on me, O God, have mercy on me," as we drop to our knees time and time again. The Canon is sung the first week of Lent, broken into pieces over the course of four nights, and then it is sung again in the fifth week of Lent, paired with the feast of St. Mary of Egypt, making for one long service with as many as two hundred prostrations.

At St. John Chrysostom, Presbytera Marion was one of two people I'd met. She was energetic and fun and married to Father Parthenios, the priest of that small Orthodox community on the west side of Nashville. Presbytera Marion went out of her way to talk with me and show me the ropes when I asked. Just before Pascha the first year after I became a catechumen, she invited me to join her for the Canon of St. Andrew, which were some of her favorite services of the Lenten season.

I struggled to find the time to attend even once that first week of Lent, and each night I missed the service because of classes or dinnertime or plans with friends or childcare issues, I felt embarrassment and I felt loss. Each night I would catch myself in the tension between real life and my budding Orthodox practice, feeling as though the two were oil and water, never able to fully become a part of one another. And each night I missed the service, I felt I was missing out on something I could not name. It felt as if the missed service would have let a long-absent part of me drop into place finally and that perhaps it was my last chance, my only chance to retrieve that absent part.

A year later, Presbytera told me again about the services. I was no less busy, no less unfocused or conflicted. I had moved back to Chicago by then, but I was in Nashville for a conference that first week of Lent, so when she reminded me of the services, I found my way there. Though I was missing the valuable networking and socializing time that might be the thing to propel my writing career just a few inches further ahead, which was the whole point of attending the conference at all, I found my way to St. John's, and the Canon was already in full swing.

I entered the cozy sanctuary mid-prostration—Have mercy on me, O God, have mercy on me. I put my things down as carefully, as quietly as possible and stood near the door, watching the company of worshippers find their way through the troparia, to the floor and back to standing—Have mercy on me, O God, have mercy on me. I listened to the sounds of the chant, the repetition of words and movements, struck by the natural cycle of things, at how easily it came to me, at how familiar it was though I'd never seen the Canon before. And I dropped to my knees then, without one hesitation—hands to the floor, my forehead touching the ground, holding there a brief moment, one inhale, one exhale, pushing myself back upright and rolling back on my heels, then pressing my fingertips into the floor to bring my body back to standing. Have mercy on me, O God, have mercy on me.

One beautiful thing about the Canon, and about all Liturgy, is that it repeats. What starts out as an interruption in the everyday, confusing and lengthy and troublesome, over time settles itself into the soul and the skin, so that without even knowing it's happening, the rhythm of it becomes a part of the participant. It sinks into us as it draws us in, until no matter where we are in the liturgical year, no matter where we are in the school calendar, no matter where we are in the fabric of our lives, we are entering in, we are a part of it all. Getting there is only the half of it; staying there in the moment and making room for it, this is the key.

This present moment is the now and the not-yet. It is the intersection of past time and present time and future time all at once. There is room for all of it there, in the kneeling, in the forehead to the ground, in the pressing to standing, the sign of the cross, Have mercy on me, O God, have mercy on me, as past regrets become present-tense redemption and future hopes become rooted in tradition as we all go marching two by two, hurrah, hurrah.

CHAPTER 15

KEEP YOU

(on belonging)

*It is only when we stand up, with all our failings and
sufferings, and try to support others rather than withdraw
into ourselves, that we can fully live the life of community.*
—Jean Vanier

My Aunt Yvonne was a talker. She was my mother's
elder sister, her only sister. When she would call the
house she would begin every conversation the same
way: "Hi, honey, I don't want to keep you." Then she spoke in
a rush, words spilling out as fast as they could come. Twenty
minutes later she'd finally ask to speak to my mother, and the
first words from her mouth to my mother inevitably would be,
"Hi, honey, I don't want to keep you."

But she did keep us.

We didn't mind, really. We liked Aunt Yvonne. She was the first to hug, the last to let go. She kept mints and gum in her purse at all times. As a teenager she looked like a young Elizabeth Taylor. Her stories were legend to us. Aunt Yvonne delighted in life, she was in constant motion, she said she didn't want to keep you but she always did keep you. One could not help but be kept.

Father Gregory called me out one night after Vespers had ended. He was making some announcements, and I was making an effort to leave. I gathered my things, slipped on my coat, and heard my name called. I looked up to see Father Gregory at the front of the quarter-full church, gesturing toward me. "Angela has been attending our Orthodoxy 101 class. I hope you'll say hello to her." Heads turned, I waved weakly. I plotted my exit strategy as the heads returned to facing front. I made my way quietly out of the pew and toward the door. A man and woman standing in the back smiled sweetly. I nodded and ducked out into the chilly Nashville night. I don't want to keep you.

It would be a lie for me to say that I don't want to keep you. I do, and I want to be kept. I want to be engaged even though it scares me. It scares me because I remember too well all the times I have kept someone in a conversation too long. I saw the signs—fidgeting, looking around the room or at the floor, shoes scuffling, waiting for a chance to bolt. A kind of panic comes over me when I feel I've stayed too long in a conversation, and I take it personally. I'm not worthy. I'm not interesting. I'm not heard. I should have started with "I don't want to keep you," but that isn't true. I do want to keep you, and I want to be kept. It's a risky thing, striking up conversation, tagging along, being the outsider trying to enter in and find her place.

Community came easy in my Catholic upbringing. We belonged to the parish drawn along lines on a map. There was no church shopping because we belonged to a street, a school, a grocery store, and a parish. We were members of St. Teresa of Avila because we lived three blocks from it and because we were Catholic. We attended church with our neighbors and our schoolmates. Belonging was simple. Identity was clear. I knew community as an extension of family, a natural outworking of my geographical location and my familial narrative.

Then I went away to college, and I was adrift, alone in a new city, immersed for the first time in an environment of moderate diversity. It was the first time I met a Protestant. He was the only other music composition major at Wright State University my freshman year. He was strait-laced and conservative. He wore a necktie; I wore a leather miniskirt, ripped fishnet tights, oversized men's dress shirt, and thrift store trench coat. He told me he was Pentecostal, and I said I'd never heard of it. I asked if that was a new religion. It was new to me. Compared to Catholicism, everything was a new religion. He was offended, and I didn't understand why.

Finding an Orthodox community in Nashville had been daunting for me. The choices were limited but remarkably different. The first time I walked into St. John Chrysostom

Orthodox Church in Nashville, I felt as though the walls were closing in on me. After spending six months attending classes at the massive Greek Orthodox Church of the Holy Trinity, I'd decided to visit St. John's. It was a rather small church, converted from a single-family home in a working-class neighborhood. I had discovered it through a friend of a friend.

I got there late and sat in my car, watching people arrive. When the steady flow of the faithful slowed to a trickle, I walked slowly to the door, trying to remember what to do first: candles, cross myself, and venerate icons. Lord have mercy, Lord have mercy, Lord have mercy. I was alone, mostly. I'd drift into the back and try to blend into the paneling or stare into the space behind the royal doors to see what Father Parthenios was doing there in the secret, hidden part of the Liturgy. When that failed I'd look at the floor, the dance of the candle flames lit on the stand, or the details of the icons nearest me on the wall. It usually worked.

I'd sneak out early, because being in the space was intimidating enough, but then having to meet and greet actual real-life humans was worse. Inside, I am true kin to Aunt Yvonne, not wanting to keep you but loving the engagement, loving the interaction. It was her courage I lacked, her surety that she had something to say that was compelling enough to keep you. I'll admit that once I know where I fit in the social structure of the space, I am more courageous, fully present and engaged. At first, though, that demon of social anxiety takes my heart in its grubby hands and squeezes it until I can't breathe, and I bolt before I have the chance to show that courage. I don't want to keep you.

Before visiting the small community of St. John's, I had this fantasy that Orthodoxy would be this unchanging set of arms waiting for me. That the structure and the ritual and the tradition would be enough to hold me, enough to keep me, but in practice that picture is a little distant. Cold concrete can't welcome me in; only flesh will answer that. And in making that realization, standing in the back of St. John's, I was gripped with the familiar anxiety of being rejected, being set apart, being the outsider once again.

It occurred to me, as I stared at the icons on the wall and the dancing of that candle flame, how often I use my fears and anxieties to get me out of feeling uncomfortable. How often do I lean on the social anxiety as a crutch, operating as if it's already part of my emotional DNA, unchangeable and final? How often do I tell it my troubles and give it another slice of my heart in the hopes that I will feel better somehow? I imagine if Jesus were in my living room and I were telling Him this, He'd say, "Throw down your crutch, you are healed," and I'd answer back, sassy-like, with "Yeah, right, easy for You to say!" And then He'd laugh, because He really does think I'm funny, but I realize too that the operative word He'd use here is "healed."

What does it look like for me to move through the injury, to bear the pain, and see what happens then? Becoming Orthodox means I cannot lie in my bed and phone in my faith; I cannot just read books or watch videos or do internet searches to inform my faith and fuel my conversion. I have to meet people, stand near, kiss the same icons and drink from the same cup. Call it an active rehab. It may always be uncomfortable to keep people. There is something to be said for discomfort. I may always be in pain. There is something to be said for pain. I may always walk with a limp. There is something to be said for those reminders of our injury.

My Aunt Yvonne died from complications of Parkinson's disease. She'd developed the illness a few years earlier, and we watched as it slowly took away her voice, her movement, her freedom. She could no longer reach out, no longer begin the embrace. She could no longer profess that she did not want to keep us, no longer fall into a rush of words spilling out as fast as they could come. It did not deter my mother from engaging my aunt. She would visit often and carry on conversations with Aunt Yvonne, knowing her well enough to be able to read her even without words.

When Aunt Yvonne finally passed away, my mother was heartbroken. She was closer to her sister than anyone else on earth. She had been the last healthy vestige of my mother's family of origin, and no matter how strange our lives became, Aunt Yvonne handled it with aplomb. She was always welcoming to us, even when we walked on her pure white living room carpet with our grubby gym shoes. She kept junk food on low shelves. She kept mints in her purse. She was outgoing and extroverted, talkative and funny. She was open and vulnerable. She was sometimes batty and always kind. She reminded us that we were welcome, that we were valued, that we were greatly loved. She kept us, and when she could no longer hold us in her wide embrace, it left a hole in the fabric of our family. My mother was heartbroken, and we were all heartbroken, because she still kept us even in her absence. One could not help but be kept.

CHAPTER 16

SUNDAY BEST

(on miniskirts and combat boots)

*To whatever church you come, observe its custom, if you
do not want to suffer or give offense.*

—St. Ambrose of Milan

*To me, punk is about being an individual
and going against the grain
and standing up and saying
"This is who I am."*

—Joey Ramone

He was shouting from across the parking lot. At first I was not sure of the words, only that they were aimed at me and that he was angry. I was angry too. I was pulling leaves from the tree near our car in the lot of Mount Saint Joseph's college. My mother was walking fast toward the Fine Arts Building and her piano lesson. I was reluctant to follow. I did not want to be there. I wanted to be at home in my room, playing or reading, anything but waiting in hard-backed chairs of the music department in that small room outside Mrs. Jablonski's studio, and so I was dragging my feet, pulling leaves from the newly planted sapling, and the man was shouting. When I stopped and turned toward him, he walked closer and shouted again so that I could make out his command: "Hey! Little boy! Stop doing that!"

It was probably the combination of brother's old jeans and T-shirt with my Dorothy Hamill haircut that led to his error, but in any case, I did not correct him. I forced my hands into my jeans pockets, turned, and walked quickly after my mother. It was the first time someone had mistaken me for a boy.

"Dress for Liturgy is Sunday Best," Janet wrote. We had never met. I was looking for a church in Chicago and a friend on the inside somewhere. It's easier with a friend on the inside. Janet was a friend of a friend in Chicago and as close as I could get to someone on the inside. The Orthodox church she recommended was further away than I'd hoped, nearly in the suburbs, but still, I considered it.

The email continued, "Men will typically wear suits and women wear skirts." I recoiled at the idea that I'd been told to wear a skirt. My inner punk rocker bristled at the idea that what defined "Sunday best" for a woman would automatically have to include a skirt. I like skirts; I don't like to be told I have to wear one. In Nashville, Father Gregory said only that dress for Liturgy was to be respectful, that some women chose to wear skirts and sometimes head coverings, but that it was my choice. St. John's was much the same. I was not happy about the suggestion from Janet, but I bit the bullet and stomped to the closet to choose something to wear my first time visiting this new Orthodox church in Chicago.

I was alone, wearing a skirt paired with my black Doc Marten combat boots. I slipped into a pew near the back, as was my habit, while I surveyed the aging congregation, the slow-moving chant, and the heavily familiar scent. I added my refrains of "Lord have mercy" to those of the people around me. I shuffled my feet in between, finding my footing, as always, overcome with the desire to fall face down to the floor, and as always distracted by my own anger and disappointment. I exited while the people moved forward to receive the Divine Mysteries, slinking to my car without seeking out Janet and without making eye contact with anyone.

When I arrived home that day, I emailed my Orthodox friends who live across at least two state lines for advice, and in that moment I felt the length of that distance. I felt alone and desperate. In the email I asked forgiveness for my self-centered notions, and I asked for their wisdom. I told them if they suggested to me that I go back, if they told me to put aside my rebellious inclinations, then I would. It sounded petty even as I typed the words, that I would throw aside a possible church home all because I was expected to wear a skirt; and yet I could not seem to let it go. Why did it matter what I wore?

I ALWAYS FELT WRIGHT STATE UNIVERSITY'S music program might have been just a little bit desperate when they took me on with my blue hair, my leopard print vest, and my moody attitude. The college orchestra was the largest group I'd ever played in. Instead of being one of two cellists, I was one of eight. I was in the last row because my playing skill was mediocre, but I earned a scholarship in music composition because my grades were good, and I'd submitted examples of songs I'd written with my application, so I must have seemed motivated.

On rehearsal days I had thirty minutes in a cramped practice room after class and then another thirty minutes before I would have to go back to my dorm, eat dinner, and change for the full orchestra. The orange miniskirt I wore that day was so tight that it made it difficult for me to sit down. I paired the skirt with a man's dress shirt, a leopard-skin vest, and a big black belt, all from the St. Vincent DePaul thrift store back home in Cincinnati.

The trumpet player whose instrument locker resided next to mine gave me a raised-eyebrow look, noticing my clothing choices, as I took the cello from my locker. I returned his look with a cold stare as he elbowed his trombone-player friend. They followed me down the crowded hallway until I reached my practice room. I shut and locked the door, and their faces filled the small window in the top of the door. I turned my chair away from the tiny window so that my back would face them and hiked up the skirt enough to place the cello between my knees.

I found the page of the Bach solo I was learning and leaned the instrument back against my chest. When I played in the orchestra, I had to adopt the posture and dress of every other player, but when I was alone, I could wear what I wanted and let my right leg drift straight out in front of my cello rather than keeping it bent alongside. I could shift the cello and move with it as I played. It was the only time I could play and feel free, running up and down the scales and letting the notes reverberate through my sternum.

I rarely wore that orange miniskirt, preferring instead dark colors, the long navy thrift store coat, the large wool men's sweaters half-eaten by moths. I would tell myself back then that I did not care how I was dressed, that I was not trying to make an impression or set myself apart, but in retrospect I know now this was always the point.

"TRY ANOTHER PLACE. TRY ONE MORE place," she suggested. I'd sought out Marcia when I first began the journey into Orthodoxy. We had never met in person; we had only electronic communications between us. I had questions I wanted answered by a modern woman in the ancient tradition. I already knew the answers I'd get from the priest or the bishop, the poet I'd met, or the male convert introduced to me at a party by mutual friend. I had questions I wanted answered by someone who had walked in my shoes and came out the other side without losing track of herself.

So I asked Marcia about the skirt wearing, about the head covering, about the arguments I felt rising against the authority of my very biology. I don't know what I had expected, some kind wisdom advising I get over myself, some harsh criticism I'd take in and let inform me going forward. I know my own short-comings, my own rebel nature, and so I gave her all the ammunition she would have needed to suggest I conform and commit. But she simply told me to try one more place, and so I agreed.

The list of Orthodox churches to choose from in Chicago was long. There was not much that made one stand out to me from another apart from a perceived ethnicity—Greek, Russian, Coptic, Ukrainian. I had already visited three churches blindly before the "Sunday best" church. I chose each of those churches based on how much I liked the name of the saint it was named after and how close it was to my house. One was too strict, one was too far, the last was too formal. I had become the Goldilocks of church searching.

I wanted Marcia to tell me to get over my pickiness. I wanted her to tell me that I was making too much of the skirt and the location and the porridge temperature—hot, cold, or otherwise. Maybe there was no "just right" when it came to church communities. I thought maybe I ought to make do and stop whining about it.

I did find one more place, close to home with a seemingly small congregation. I searched out the faces in the pictures from their website. It looked modern, diverse, and welcoming, even if it did have poor parking options. Before I attended that one more place, I located something in myself, some small shred of hope I'd managed to hide away—not the rebellious and reactionary girl who had to be noticed, who had to be different, but instead something soft and strong, some thread of hope I barely knew existed.

For too many years I had come to rely on the idea of being accepted as canon testimony to my value. I thought somehow that if I was interesting enough, smart enough, wild enough, mysterious enough, I would be accepted, I would be loved, I would be valuable. I tried to see trying one more place as an act of hope rather than an exercise in futility. I tried to approach it not out of resignation but out of trust. I needed to trust; I was too tired to fight.

I had laid no groundwork for the visit. I did not email the priest, I did not ask anyone about wearing a skirt or a head-covering, and although I wore the skirt anyway, I left my combat boots at home, because it was warm outside and they were heavy, and I was tired of the heaviness, tired of the heat, tired of the battle.

I arrived at Christ the Savior Orthodox Church just in time for the start of the Trisagion, the "thrice holy," a standard hymn in the Divine Liturgy. I arrived to hear the choir's voices as they filtered through the archway, "Holy God." Drifting past the icons, past the murals of the martyrs on the walls, "Holy Mighty." Summoning the stories of the saints with whom I had only recently become passingly familiar, "Holy Immortal." The harmonies washed over me, my hands, my chest, my bare legs below my knee-length jersey skirt, "Have mercy on us."

I stood rooted to the spot as I found my voice in this, my favorite part of the Liturgy. I made the sign of the cross then, quietly adding myself to the prayer and entering in, struck by the thought that everywhere in the world where Liturgy occurs at this moment, we were all entering in, we were all having this moment, no matter what we wore, what we thought, what we did for a living, what our history or our future; we were all entering in here and now, "in the name of the Father and the Son and the Holy Spirit, now and ever, unto ages of ages, Amen. . . . Holy Immortal, have mercy on us."

The Trisagion welcomed me in as I remembered that this was the feeling I'd been after all along, this was the reason I came. I was home then, because something had burned away, something I no longer needed. The questioning and the rebellion would always be in me, part of my behavioral makeup, but the resentment and the fear had burned away in that moment for reasons I could not understand and could not define. And it no longer mattered whether I wore a skirt or a head covering or a leopard-skin vest, heavy black belt, and combat boots. It was never about what I wore.

CHAPTER 17

TOUCH

(on kissing—icons and otherwise)

*A kiss is a lovely trick designed by nature to stop speech
when words become superfluous.*

—Ingrid Bergman

*There is some kiss we want
with our whole lives,
the touch of spirit on the body.*

—Rumi

I French-kissed my boyfriend in church, during Mass, when
I was fifteen. I didn't mean to do it. Honestly.

He was my first boyfriend and the first guy I had
ever kissed. I had watched way too many romantic movies in

preparation for this first kiss that day at the drive-in. Andy was a band geek at a boy's high school across town. We met at parties or mixers or the 7/11 parking lot or anywhere underage kids could gather. He asked me to the drive-in for a date, but I suggested doubling, so my friend Diane tagged along, and Andy rustled up a date for her from his band pals. The movie was a summer blockbuster, car chase, thriller, and at a quiet point in the film, he leaned over the stick shift and bucket seats and planted that first kiss. It was uncomfortable and awkward, the bucket seat and stick shift pressing into my ribcage, the smell of his acne medication filling the air, the sound of Diane and Andy's friend Paul alternately giggling and making out behind us. It was cliché, but it was my story even so.

It was only a few weeks into our dating relationship that I invited him to church with me. It might have been a baptism or a wedding. Though I don't know how he came to be standing next to me at Mass that afternoon, I do remember that in the early part of our short dating experience, we spent a lot of time making out. I think it might have been the bulk of our dating relationship. It took me by surprise when he leaned over to kiss me on the lips during the Sign of Peace, and I guess conditioning took over from our summer drive-in escapades, and I went all Pavlov's dogs on him. He broke off right away and covered for us. No one noticed apart from the two of us and probably God. Pretty sure God caught that. I think my face remained red for about three years every time the Sign of Peace floated in, long after that dating relationship stopped.

The bounds of affection were so blurry for me then. I didn't see a kiss from a boy as a sign of affection or trust or even romance. It wasn't that I didn't enjoy the kissing; certainly, I did. In retrospect, though, I can see how much it was more a method to please him, to keep him interested, to satisfy some requirement of love and commitment. This is what one does next. But his kiss hello and the kiss goodbye never felt much different to me from the making out in the car at the drive-in, and that was an important distinction—even if the lesson had to come in front of God, the priest, and everyone.

Entering into a religious practice that incorporates the body and spirit with such intention and such intensity has been a whole world of awkward for me. There is an awful lot of kissing in the Orthodox tradition—icons, priests' and bishops' rings, crosses, fellow travelers. In addition to the intimacy of the act, the when, where, who, and how of each kiss is often what trips me up.

By the time we arrived back in Chicago, I was already tweaked about knowing what to do and when to do it, because while in Nashville, at the start of my catechism, I had the chance to meet the metropolitan for our region. It took me by surprise, and so when I met him I felt at a complete loss. I didn't know what to do, and I was first to greet him in our small group, so I had no one to model it for me. I was half inclined to high-five the guy, I was so befuddled. Also, in my own defense, he wasn't wearing his "bling." He wasn't totally in his civvies, but he was certainly dressed down at that moment. In the end I just shook his hand and told him I was honored to meet him. Then I stepped aside and backed out of the room as quickly and silently as I could.

A couple of years later, when we were settled in Chicago, I happened to see our bishop in the hall at the church on a day I was supposed to meet with Father John. I admit, I pretended I had not seen him. I turned quickly to go in the opposite direction. I don't think he noticed. Later, in my car, I rehearsed what I might have said or done if I had met him again, remembering my meeting with the metropolitan in Nashville and wanting to get it right this time. Father John had explained to me before the guidelines for greeting clergy, so in the car I considered what I was supposed to have said. "Master, bless," I voiced to no one in particular, and then I shook my head. It was so awkward, so unfelt. I could not wrap my head around it.

In the Orthodox tradition, greetings to the clergy are meant to convey respect for the most part, and though I do respect the clergy, the act of kissing the ring of a man I did not know felt off somehow. The feminist in me had a panic attack at the mere thought of it. It may be, though, that it's not the humbling act of asking for a blessing or even kissing his ring. It is simply that the act is so personal, so familiar. I was not sure what was expected of me. I did not want to do it wrong, and at the same time I did not want to miss out on something important. Yet I simply could not complete the act; I did not know what it meant to me. Having brushed up against my social anxiety issues mixed with the therapy I'd done on boundary issues, I knew I needed time to discern that act and see it from outside myself rather than through the lens of the girl who wanted to do it right, the girl who was afraid to sing the words to that Billy Joel song because she wanted to be good and not die young.

Usually, I would let my sons leave Liturgy after the dismissal before people would line up to venerate the cross. I let them run next door to find the coffee cake and juice they only saw here at fellowship. It had become a treat for having been good during the service. Good was a relative term in our clan, usually meaning that if they had to lie on the ground and pout about being bored during Liturgy, they'd do it out of earshot and eyesight of Father John.

I asked, once, that they stay and venerate the cross with me. I explained to them the procedure: wait in line, step forward, accept the blessing of the priest, and then kiss the cross and the priest's ring. They were unsure, as if they were being asked to kiss Great Aunt Betty, who talks too loud and smells like cigarettes and cabbage. They don't know Great Aunt Betty, why are they offering a gift so great to this person they do not know? To them, the act has some sacrifice. To them, it was awkward, unfelt, and I understood that. I wanted to wait then, until they had some connection to the cross, some desire to venerate, and until I could give them the missing pieces, offer some guidance and instruction on it. The trouble is, they might never care to show affection to Great Aunt Betty, and so the line to venerate the cross never willingly included the boys. They had no desire to do so, no curiosity towards it.

After nearly a year of attendance, I sent them off to fellow-ship and stood in line as usual. A moment later they came back: "That man said we should get in line and venerate the cross." I looked to the door, and Nick lifted a hand to wave and smile. He was a nice cradle Orthodox man we'd met when we first arrived at the church. I nodded and waved back. Well, if Nick said that, then it's time perhaps, I thought. I told the boys to stand in line; I instructed them quickly on what to do. No one complained. We didn't talk about it again that day.

The following week when Liturgy ended, I picked up my bag and got into line to venerate the cross. Nick was not there. The boys looked to me and pointed to the door, but I shook my head. "Let's do this first," I said. They stood in line, whisper-ing only once to me to remind them of what to do. When we were done, they ran next door, never mentioning a word about it. This is just what we do now, I thought.

I make it too hard. I over-explain. I expect disagreement. I plan for disaster. I project my own discomfort, my forty-plus years of awkwardness and rejection and judgment and rebellion, onto these four children, and sometimes, because God is good, they surprise me by shirking it off and finding their own way. Despite my best efforts at sabotage, they find a way to integrate new things into themselves and find their own connections to it.

I keep expecting that one day I'll just get a rejection letter in the mail: "Dear Catechumen, thank you so much for your inter-est in the Orthodox Church; however, your application does not fit our community at this time." Becoming chrismated seems to stand out as a way to diffuse the awkward, to let go of the idea that I'm constantly being tested and constantly found lacking. But in letting myself make Orthodoxy into some kind of high judge, waiting for my mistakes, I do it the worst disservice. I set it up according to my own historical experiences with failure. I set myself up to fail again and again and again. It is a recipe for disappointment.

Becoming Orthodox, or rather, becoming chrismated, is the commitment. To fulfill the promise my godparents made for me when I was baptized as an infant in the Catholic Church has come to mean a final acceptance, a final determination that I am welcome no matter how often I do it wrong, no matter how many mistakes I make. I find that I was wrong. I am Great Aunt Betty—it is I who married into the family, who shows up at Thanksgiving dinner singing the wrong songs and saying outrageous things, wearing shoes too small and dresses too large, kissing on both cheeks, sometimes on the mouth, hugging too long or not long enough. And yet everyone loves that Aunt Betty once they get to know her. Everyone forgives her missteps and her sloppy kisses, everyone welcomes her when she arrives, and no one wants her to go. There's room for us all at the table.

CHAPTER 18

PRONE TO WANDER

(on feeling homeless)

*The ache for home lives in all of us, the safe place where
we can go as we are and not be questioned.*
— Maya Angelou

I have always felt a little homeless. It's a strange thing.
— Annie Lennox

J esus doesn't care about your parking space. I'm convinced
of this. Jesus doesn't care about your parking space, and
I doubt that Jesus ever took St. Christopher's word into
consideration, even before the Catholic Church fired him and
took him off the "safe driving" account. I was tempted to say
this to my band mate when she prayed out loud for somewhere

to park after we moved into the packed-out Wrigleyville neighborhood of Chicago.

She was the only one in our band who had a car in Chicago. When she came home to tell us she'd gotten a car from her boyfriend, everyone was eager to take a ride, to go further than we'd gone before, to have a way to get our equipment to and from our short list of gigs. But parking in our Wrigleyville neighborhood was scarce, and we'd circle for long stretches of time if the parking spot behind the apartment was taken. I'd stay in the car with her while she circled, and we'd smoke her cigarettes, because she had a full-time job and I was always "trying to quit." I'd keep her company and watch the same scenery pass by, looking for the telltale sign of movement, headlights coming on, brake lights blinking. When a spot opened up finally, I would thank God, not because I thought Jesus had engineered the space, but because I was tired of the circling, I only wanted to be home.

I usually took the train home from school or work even when she offered me a ride, because it was quick, direct, prescribed. I would take the clacking of the train on the track over the start and stop of the traffic any day. I could think on the train, the stops were clear, the seats, when available, were usually clean. I knew where I was going when I took the train. I knew where I'd been.

When I was a kid and we'd lose things, we'd chant, "Tony, Tony look around, something's lost and can't be found," in the hope that St. Anthony, patron saint of lost things, would shine a magical beam of light on the missing object. When what was missing was inside of us and we felt desperate and alone, we'd pray to St. Jude, patron saint of lost causes. If we were inclined toward music, we were instructed to pray to St. Cecelia, patron saint of music and musicians. We took it a step further with poor St. Joseph; we buried statues of him in the yards of houses we were trying to sell. St. Joseph, patron of carpenters and workers, stepdad to Jesus, long-suffering. He was quick to act when a dream tipped him off about the soldiers who came looking for his infant son, and now we'd bury statues of him in our yard in the hopes of selling property.

The saints I knew opened windows when God closed doors, stepped in when things were dire, sat in the passenger seat and kept us safe while driving. The idea I came away with was that we had someone on the inside putting in a good word for us. When God felt unreachable, we could call on the intercession of the saints or the Virgin Mary. They were the advocates for us, and they all had their appointed areas of expertise. I liked having this compartmentalized for me. Though the Vatican didn't sanction the more superstitious aspects of this, this daily living out of the faith held long and held true. We learned church doctrine in our religion classes at St. Teresa, but we learned how to live as Catholics from our heritage, our family members, and our neighbors.

By the time we'd been attending Orthodox Liturgy for about a year, my kids had developed their own particular rituals for navigating the long service. It was probably the only time during the week they were required to be still and quiet for a ninety-minute chunk of time. Riley staggered her bathroom visits to break up the time, Chet drew, Miles wedged himself into a corner near the back and scowled at people. But my middle son Henry would wander around, staring at the murals and the icons. He was quiet and respectful, so I didn't stop him. Once in a while he'd come back and report to me what he'd discovered.

Henry was absent most of the Liturgy one Sunday, wandering around the nave and the narthex, as he was known to do. After a length of time I went to look for him, to be sure he hadn't gotten lost in what felt like a maze of catacombs in the basement of the building. I found him in the narthex staring at the mural of St. Xenia, listening as Christopher, a church friend, explained the saint's story, that St. Xenia was a widow, that she became a "fool for Christ." Henry stared at the mural, taking that in, listening then questioning, quietly. The mural of St. Xenia painted in the narthex of Christ the Savior is hard to miss. She greets visitors, standing just above and to the left of the icon of Christ. I spotted her the first time I entered the church, waiting for my turn to venerate the icon.

I recognized Xenia's name only because my first college was in Fairborn, which was near Xenia, Ohio. We pronounced it Zeen-yah, and as far as I knew, its claim to fame was that it seemed to be a sort of tornado magnet. Springtime at Wright State University brought the storm warnings I was used to, having been raised in the Miami Valley, but it seemed as though Xenia always got the worst of it. The town was named for the

Greek word meaning "hospitality," but the Native Americans had always called it "the place of the devil wind."

My dorm room was on the first floor and had concrete walls with windows facing a courtyard, so during tornado warnings I'd stay in my room, watching as much of the sky as I could see, watching for the green overlay that came when a tornado was brewing. The sirens came from the nearby Wright Patterson Air Force Base, so they were especially loud.

Tornado warnings never scared me. I didn't worry about what could happen; I didn't worry at all. It was perhaps the only time I felt some sense of peace, letting go the future and the past, living just in that moment. I'd seen a tornado once, from the picture window at my Aunt Yvonne's house. We watched as the sky grew black and the sirens wailed. The clouds above the tornado were grey and green, expansive as they penetrated the sky around them. The funnel was long and skinny, like a string dancing and swaying. We watched the tornado for a long time, having no idea what destruction it caused, seeing only the massive beauty and power it commanded there through the picture window, and I felt peaceful. I felt respectful, knowing nature was not evil, it was simply itself, doing what it had done long before men decided to place houses and schools and car washes in its path.

After a long time of watching the slow-moving cloud, my uncle ushered us to the basement quickly, telling us it was hard to predict the path of tornados, that though it looked like it would miss us, we couldn't be sure, and that even from here the winds could send debris though that glass. So we sat on the floor in their basement, in the dark, listening to the wind outside and the battery-operated radio at our feet, hiding from a force of nature.

Though I had not known St. Xenia's story, my first thought on seeing her name was for tornados, the storms coming, remembering watching the sky turn colors, and the waiting. Time stopped during a tornado warning as time stopped for me when I would enter the narthex for Divine Liturgy. Henry had never mentioned the mural to me before, and I never thought to bring it up. Though I knew most of the Catholic saints, I did not recognize many of those painted on the walls and resting on the icon stands.

In the Orthodox tradition as with Catholics, the saints also have areas of assignment. As in Catholicism, they are patrons. St. Xenia of St. Petersburg is the patron saint of employment, marriage, the homeless, fires, missing children, and spouses. St. Xenia wandered the streets of St. Petersburg for forty-five years, sometimes wearing her deceased husband's military uniform, proclaiming Christ to anyone who would listen. She wandered about doing good works, sometimes appearing crazy, always a force of nature, unstoppable.

At the stoplight near the intersection of Western and Chicago avenues a woman walks, smiling constantly, with closed lips and sad, kind eyes. She is beautiful, carrying an old Styrofoam coffee cup, shaking it as she walks between the cars day after day. I drive this route to drop Henry at school each morning at this time, and I see her, always smiling, walking slowly no matter the weather. When it's snowing or raining, she pulls a hood up over her long hair, but the smile does not leave her face. She is neither young nor old, her beauty being ageless, and it transcends her station, her poverty, her addictions, her sadness. She shakes the cup, making eye contact only briefly, long enough to make the connection but not long enough to inflict nor to collect shame.

A man who had no legs broke me of giving money to homeless people in Chicago a long time ago. I walked down Michigan Avenue near Columbia College on my way to class. The transition from Xenia, Ohio, to Chicago was a welcome culture shock; the wind was stronger, the atmosphere dangerous, but not deadly to me. I was never afraid of Mother Nature, but human nature was terrifying, and I kept to myself as I navigated public transportation, walking quickly from one place to another, never making eye contact.

At the crosswalk one day, as I waited for the light to change, a man in a wheelchair approached me. I'd seen him there before and had managed to avoid him. He caught me there, waiting, and told me the short version of his story, that he was a veteran, that he'd lost his legs in the war. He told me he needed twenty-two dollars to stay the night at the YMCA on Chicago Avenue. He asked me for the money, and though I told him I did not have it, he asked again, framing his request with more detailed information about the stay. He said if I gave him my address, he'd send the money back.

I opened my purse and offered the three dollars I had there, the only cash I carried. I showed him my wallet and explained that I was a student. He shook his head and pushed away the three dollars. "That won't get me nothing," he said. The light had now changed twice as I tried to explain again that I didn't have the money. He shook his head, disgusted with me, swearing at me or at the situation, his failure or mine, I don't know. He wheeled himself away quickly, still swearing, as I stood on the corner holding three dollars in my hand, my purse still open, shaken and confused as something shifted in me. It was the last time I offered to give money to someone on the street.

When the homeless woman with the beautiful smile passed my car at the stoplight the first day on the way to school, Henry asked if I would give her money. It had been a long time since the thought had even crossed my mind. I had gotten into the habit of looking away; to ease my conscience, I'd pray silently for them, make mental notes to bolster my contributions to charities as I tried to looked busy, important, distracted. When Henry suggested it, I caught her eye, and she looked away but kept smiling. I took note of her clothing, her hair, and her cup, rattling as she passed his window, until the light changed and I could drive away.

Henry had asked me before about people who were homeless, and I would answer with my usual response that we should pray, that we don't know their situation, that we shouldn't judge. He asked if I thought we'd ever be homeless, and though I assured him that a lot would have to happen to find us in that situation, the question struck something, some homesickness, some homelessness I carried in me.

In the last thirty years I've moved fourteen times, sometimes to a new city, sometimes just to a new apartment or house. The process never becomes easier, even as I get better at house hunting, at packing, at finding places to put things. The newness wears off more quickly, the things that break in the process of moving are always surprising, the transition from one home to another is daunting.

In the last twenty years I have moved churches fourteen times, sometimes in a new city, sometimes just a new denomination or satellite location. The process never becomes easier, no matter how skilled I am at church hunting, at packing my theology and my quirks, at finding places to stand, sit, or kneel. The things that break in the process of moving churches are always surprising, always painful, always daunting, and the feeling of being poorly rooted, of being homeless, always seemed to hang overhead somehow. Having a sense of place has always felt transient and maybe dangerous, like building a house in the place of the devil wind, renaming that place Hospitality. Or like walking barefoot through town, being vulnerable, labeled crazy, and holding the sweet, sad smile that marks us forever as homeless, as needy, as hopeful.

CHAPTER 19

Prayer and Practice

(on being consistent)

A jug fills drop by drop.

—Buddha

A small but always persistent discipline is a great force;
for a soft drop falling persistently hollows out hard rock.

—St. Isaac of Syria

Thinking out loud one day at coffee with some old friends and Doreen, a woman I had just met, I mentioned my idea that one does not often meet disgruntled Buddhists. I wondered, still aloud, why that was. Maybe I just don't know enough Buddhists.

Doreen answered that as a Buddhist herself she knew quite

a few friends who had "fallen away." She explained that it was not usually caused by some injustice or power struggle with a leader or a community, but in her estimation, the world was just too loud, too compelling, too strong. Those who fall out of practice don't run from the practice as much as their time is just consumed by kids' baseball games or mortgage payments, by the rough job market or the entertainment options. American life is not conducive to religions that require a "practice."

I resonated with this. My children are attending four different schools; my work is freelance and sporadic. My social life is disjointed, and my workouts are hit or miss. Time is essential. Time is slippery, like water sliding through and seeping into the soil until it's gone, making everything mud and then evaporating into the air.

I have to start early with the reminders and the cajoling every day. It's my job to be this drill sergeant, this one-woman pep squad, keeper of the daily to-do list. I'm barking out orders to get dressed, put on shoes, eat the food on the table, get books, go to the car, brush teeth, carry out the trash. I have to repeat myself two, three, maybe four times, and often I sound as though I'm stuck on a loop. By the third time I've repeated myself, I am agitated and I can feel the lines around my lips dig deeper in my trademark Grinch frown, eyebrows pressed together in a look of perpetual disapproval. They'll ask me then, when my next reminder is sharp and loud, if I'm angry, and I admit to it. I am angry. I don't like being the human to-do list. I don't like this part of the job. I like the part of the job that involves affirmation and hugs. I like the part in which I am given the gold and glimmering "best mom in the world" trophy. I feel ignored, unimportant, ineffectual when I am reduced to barking out orders hour after hour.

My priest is like the dentist. I told him this one week at our meeting. He is the dentist. I recognize his authority to inform me of spiritual things, to help me find ways to clean that dirty nous, to be in right relationship with my Creator and with my community. He'll tell me to floss because it's important. He'll tell me to look into that sonic toothbrush, he'll recommend a root canal, and I will listen. But I won't floss. I just know that I am not going to floss no matter how much I know that he is right and that my gums are receding before my very eyes. I just won't make time for it.

I recognize his authority to ask it of me, and I told him this. We all know he's right and it's his job to tell us to floss, to pray, to attend, but often we won't do it, and it will frustrate him because he'll know how helpful it is. I told him he should expect that I'll feel overwhelmed and out of control where time is concerned. I told him he should expect that when he tells me to floss, often, I will not listen. It doesn't mean I don't hear him, and it doesn't mean I don't agree it's the right thing. It just means I am making other choices at the moment.

AFTER COMMUNION IN THE CATHOLIC MASS I liked to watch the priest as he gathered the elements back onto the altar. The priest was in the open now, unlike in years past when he faced away from the people as he performed his ritual tasks, his liturgical housekeeping around communion. Vatican II opened everything up and made it public. I would watch as the priest took the *diskos* and the chalice, lifting, blessing, consuming all that was left of the wine, placing the remainder of the consecrated bread in the tabernacle in the alcove to his left. Each action was done with precision, prayer—the practice always the same time after time. I liked to think of it as doing the dishes, cleaning up after the feast. It fascinated me to watch this ritual cleanup; it was calm and orderly, and it meant we were nearly done, ready to move forward into the great unknown of our weekly lives. The acts were symbolic yet utilitarian. They are ordinary actions, things I do every day of my life in practice, small domestic tasks—and yet if they are left undone, the effect is felt.

After I'd heard Scott Cairns read his work at the writer's conference in Michigan and speak about his journey into Orthodoxy, I purchased a chotki, or prayer rope, to wear on my wrist. It was years before I ever considered becoming Orthodox, but I bought the prayer rope because I worried all the time, and I thought it might help me to set aside the worry, that it would remind me to pray when its rough yarn brushed against my wrist. I bought it, but I did not wear it. The prayer rope sat in my jewelry box and languished there with the rest of the contents—necklaces I never wore, rings that did not fit, prayer cards from my grandmothers' funerals, teeth collected from my parental tooth fairy duties.

I bought my oldest son a prayer rope one Sunday after Liturgy because he was worried and he did not know what to do with himself. That day at Liturgy he'd fidget and shoot forlorn looks in my direction. He was twelve and already a world-class worrier. He came by it naturally. He lit four candles. He stared at them and sighed, blowing out several others in the process. He looked at me and sighed again. When he returned to me, I wrapped my arms around him, because I did not know what else to do. It was about his computer, and while I felt angry that he'd spend that much energy on the thing, I did not let the anger show. Instead, I wrapped my arms around him and held him close. I did this often in Liturgy, for each of my children. When they were bored or distracted or lonely or angry, I'd wrap my arms around them and hold them, because it made me feel as though we had some anchoring then, or at least some comfort. Even if I did not like the reasons for their worry, their pouting, their emotion, I could set aside my judgment and be fully present to them.

Chet ran his finger over the rough yarn of the prayer rope on my wrist. He looked at me and smiled a bit, so I took it off, and without a word, I slipped it over his skinny hand. He smiled again. I kissed him on his cheek, and he wore the prayer rope for a few minutes. When the time was right, I whispered to him that when he felt worried he should feel the prayer rope on his wrist and let that remind him to pray about it, to let it go. I told him that when he felt worried, he should hold the rope in his hands and say the Jesus Prayer, stare ahead at the candles he'd lit, and breathe deep, let it go, trust that worry was not something he needed to carry. It was too heavy for him, too big for him to fight. It was his giant in the road. He nodded in that earnest way he has, and he wore the prayer rope the rest of the service. At the end of Liturgy, he handed it back to me. He thanked me for it, and I asked if he'd like one for himself. He nodded again, smiling, thankful and eager again.

Tom Waites plays my favorite version of Satan in the movie *The Imaginarium of Dr. Parnassus.* He is gritty and persistent. He is charming without being classically handsome, and he is compelling in his logic while trying to sway Dr. Parnassus from the straight and narrow path of the monk. In an early part of the movie, he visits Dr. Parnassus in a cave where monks are telling "the eternal story." He scoffs at the idea that what keeps the world turning is this telling and this story, so he silences the monks one at a time, because this much he can do. He closes their mouths one after another until finally the cave is silent. He holds up his hands to Dr. Parnassus, exuberant that he has proved his point. He goads the Doctor, "Cheer up—I've freed you from this ridiculous nonsense."

An eagle suddenly swoops into the enormous cave, and Dr. Parnassus jumps up, jubilant. The devil is confused, but Dr. Parnassus explains, "A sign! A message! That bird was a messenger—from distant places we know not of! Other places! The point is, you're wrong! And I'm wrong! It doesn't have to be us here! Somewhere in the world, at any given time, someone is telling the story! Sustaining the universe! Right now, it's happening. That's why we're still here. You can't stop stories being told somewhere! You can't be everywhere!"

There was a moment during Liturgy when this scene came to me. As I watched the priest perform his tasks, listened to the congregation move through the litany of "Lord have mercy," inhaled the scent of the incense, I had this moment in which I realized that what we do there is to tell the eternal story, the story without which there is nothing. It is at times mechanical, at times mystical. At any given moment in a congregation such as mine, there are participants who lack focus or faith or fortitude, but as I stood in the Liturgy this week I realized that somewhere there is always someone telling this story—and that perhaps, as Orthodox Christians, this is what we do in Divine Liturgy. We tell the eternal story, consistently week after week.

For some people, this practice, this act, seems foolish, a waste of time and energy. It seems rote and maybe superstitious, perhaps worthless and boring, but this is part of what drew me first to becoming Orthodox. That this ancient practice still exists in a modern world, informing the lives of the people who perform the tasks, say the prayers, and light the candles week after week, is remarkable and miraculous. And whether I am there at Liturgy or not, the story is being told, and when I am there, I am engaging in the telling. And if I'm doing it well, this eternal story reaches out into the wideness of my life, not stopping on the steps of the church as I leave each week. When I pray at home, I am engaging in the telling. When I am in the grocery store, I am engaging in the telling. When I am caring for my children or my husband or supporting the health of my body, I am engaging in the telling of that eternal story. This is the prayer. This is the practice.

So when I am flustered or discouraged, I comfort myself with the idea that no matter what the event or location, there is something happening in the telling of that story at a level we cannot even know, that mystical moment during which we connect with something outside of ourselves, the voice of someone always telling the eternal story, the story without which there is nothing.

PART III

INTO THE ROAR

Only through struggle can we acquire humility.
—Abbot Tryphon of Christ the Saviour
Monastery, Vashon Island, WA

There is an old African story about lions. When the lions reach a certain advanced age, they become slow and cannot catch the gazelles as easily. Their manes are bushy and majestic, and their roar is fierce, but their teeth are no longer sharp and deadly. The young lions are fast, and their bite is lethal, but they are not quite fast enough to catch the gazelles. So the old lions lie in the tall grass when the hunt begins and wait, in hiding. The young lions begin to chase the gazelles, getting them just within reach; the gazelles' pace outstrips that of the young lions, so the young lions herd them toward the tall grass where the older lions wait. When the gazelles come close, the old lions let out their terrible roars, filling the grassland with sound and fury. This frightens the gazelles, who turn to run away, straight into the advancing line of young lions. The moral being—don't be afraid of what you cannot see. Run into the roar.

After the giants in the road—the things I could see from a long way off, the blocks in the road that were visible and tangible—there were lions on my road to becoming Orthodox. In the tall grass ahead, there were fears and doubts and difficulties I could not articulate with any success. From the start, the journey into Orthodoxy was filled with giants in the road, obstacles I could see, and in some way I could navigate those battles. I knew where those fears began. I could make a plan, sway and move, bob and weave my way if I wanted to get around those giants. But past that now, from the tall grass came terrifying roars and the desire to turn and run.

Sometimes I understand my own fears and doubts; I can see what stops me from moving forward. Social anxiety, fear of disappointing someone, fear of doing it wrong—those are things I know how to handle. But roaring from the bushes ahead, the places I could not see into, stopped me just as easily, and in that my aim of becoming Orthodox was revealed to be a dash to the long grass. In some ways it had become a desire to find a hiding place from the world, from my own inadequacy, from the future I cannot see or control. The tall grass as the goal shows itself to hold all the same fears and doubts, the roar of lions ahead, the sight of lions in pursuit. Everywhere there are lions, life or death, and the choice then becomes narrow: turn away or run into the roar.

CHAPTER 20

THEODORA

(on being named)

Each generation wants new symbols, new people, new names. They want to divorce themselves from their predecessors.

—Jim Morrison

If we have no peace, it is because we have forgotten that we belong to each other.

—Mother Teresa

I'm pretty sure Adam named the animals because he was lonely. He woke in the Garden, surrounded by life yet absent a common spoken language with it. The implication is, of course, that he was able to speak to God and that God responded; but the life that teemed around him was visceral, tangible, and so he named the animals, because that's what we do when we're lonely. We name things. Without names we're more aware of how alone we feel. Without names we have no context, no relevance, no relationship, and so Adam took care of that. He was a problem-solver from the start.

My Aunt Vicky's voice always sounded too loud for her short stature. She was raven-haired, brash, married to my dad's closest brother in age. Uncle Kenny was only a year and some change younger than my dad, and they looked so alike to me, I could imagine them as twins. From across the room at my grandmother's house, Aunt Vicky called my name, and so I turned to answer—but she was not talking to me. I should have known it; I was only called Angela when I was in trouble. Everyone called me Angie. It was the first time I understood that I shared my name with my grandmother.

When I introduced myself to strangers, telling them my name, which was rare, I would mumble. People would think I was saying "Nancy" instead of "Angie," and sometimes I was too embarrassed to correct them, though it wasn't my mistake.

Almost everyone in my friend circles had nicknames when I was a kid. My friend Bonnie was Biff, Margaret was Hex, Denise was Dex. Apart from using Angie instead of Angela, there was not much they could do with my name, and so I was the only one without a cool nickname. They tried to throw new names out there, but nothing really stuck.

The closest I came was in the eighth grade, when I played

softball for one season. I got caught smoking a cigarette behind a friend's garage with my cousin and her friends. It got back to the team captains, so when they put names on our jerseys, they wrote "Nicki" on mine—short for Nicotine Woman, I was told. At first, I tried to play it off, to live into the bad girl label I'd never worn before. But in the end it just felt like an attempt to tear me down, to tweak my familiar Catholic guilt and to point a finger at the weird kid who played softball badly and sometimes smoked menthol cigarettes with her cousin behind a friend's garage.

My grandmother had her own version of a nickname. We called her Muzzie. She had wild, tufted hair done in some warm shade of blonde, even into her seventies. Well-dressed and willowy, she owned every room she entered. No matter whom I ask about it, no one seems to know where the name started, only that it's what she was called and that she liked it. Her given name was Verna Jean, and I'm Angela Jean, after both grandmothers.

All of us, my siblings and I, are named for family members on one side of the family or the other. The year I was confirmed as a Catholic, I was in the eighth grade. Even my confirmation name was given to me. It was a "Marian year" in our parish, and girls were encouraged to take a name to honor the Virgin Mary; so I was Marie. Angela Jean Marie Doll. All of my names belonged to someone else, and all of them were chosen for me in one way or another.

When I was pregnant the first time, Dave and I paged through the three baby name books I'd bought the moment we discovered I was pregnant. I had gone through once already, circling the names I liked, choosing them because they fit with Carlson and because they had a meaning that spoke to me.

Inevitably, the names I liked most, Dave hated. He wanted something bold, something that would stand out. I wanted something subtle, something different but easy to say, easy to remember. When he suggested Kingfish for a boy, I laughed, but he was serious. It came from the story of the Fisher King. In the Arthurian legend, the Fisher King is also called the "wounded" king. He guards the Holy Grail. Having lost the use of his legs and unable to move on his own, he is reduced to sitting by the river and fishing. His healing can only come at the hands of a mystical knight, a "chosen" one who will bring the king back to full health. In the story, it is only the Grail that keeps the Fisher King alive.

I rejected Dave's suggestion based first on the name itself— one that Dave suggested a kid could "grow into." I contended it was a name a kid could get pounded on the playground over. After reading the story that informed the name, we both realized the mythology of that name carried too heavy a backstory, too painful a heritage. Though we agreed the mythology did not fit with our hopes for our future daughter, he suggested it with each subsequent pregnancy anyway, just to keep me on my toes, I think.

In the Orthodox tradition, we are named. Father Gregory suggested that St. Angelina might be a good patron saint. It was the closest he could come to my given name. He also suggested that St. Anna might suffice. I asked about the rules of naming, about what was allowed, about the meaning and the purpose of it. I knew other converts who had taken new names because their own names had no correlation to an Orthodox saint, but I wanted a new name, and I wanted to choose my patron based not on the person I had always been but on the person I wanted to be. Father Gregory shrugged pleasantly. "It's up to you." It was the first time I felt as though it was up to me.

I arrived at Theodora because I'd been searching for stories of the saints, the Desert Mothers and the Ammas. I gravitated toward St. Sophia at first, the name meaning "wisdom" and the concept being one I reached for with open, grasping hands every time I felt I had said or done something stupid, which was often. But St. Sophia's main gig, so far as I could tell, was that she was the mother of three daughters, Faith, Hope, and Charity, and that they were all martyred. And though I reached for Wisdom, taking Sophia's name didn't feel right. I wanted something new, something untried. If I was going to share another name, then I wanted to choose something that resonated in me, as a string vibrates with sound when plucked. So I turned my attention back to the saints, the Desert Mothers and the Ammas, and there was Theodora of Vasta, sitting in the results of my web search engine when I looked for another Mrs. Metaphor.

When my friend David Bunker spoke, the room would go silent, and he would ramble and riff on whatever theological or philosophical topic had been tossed into the middle of the room. Women in leadership, music as worship, commercial applications of ancient religious practices and our massive judgment of mega church culture—whatever came up, Dave B. had his own unique and deeply metaphorical perspective. He was profound and kind and wise, and we'd all listen, calling him Mr. Metaphor because of his tendency to show how things were related, how we were all related. It is probably because of David Bunker that I began to draw those connections in my own writing. Metanoia was my first experience with a postmodern nondenominational church plant, and Dave Bunker was my first non-Catholic spiritual father.

In metaphor there is no soft comparison, there is no implication that one thing is like something else. This leaves too much space, too much wiggle room. Metaphor is strong; the Greeks define it as a kind of "crossing over," just as the elements of the Divine Mysteries, the bread and wine, make this crossing. They are bread and wine, and they are also the body and blood. They are a bridge and the crossing, and we are the bridge and the crossing over.

The internet was still young and the trend of online web logs was new when I jumped on the blogging bandwagon. I adopted the name of Mrs. Metaphor. The first year was struggle and wrestling with big questions. I admit, the more I tried to be the voice of authority and wisdom and truth, the more pretentious I sounded. Over time, I stopped trying to teach, stopped trying too hard, stopped trying to be someone else. Over time, I found the soft sweet spot I needed, the genuine voice I'd been after and then lost and then found again. It was wandering in the woods, remembering there was a beautiful place there I'd found once but could not put on a map. I could only enter the woods and find it by feel. The more I traveled there, the better I became at finding it, no matter how the leaves or the weather or my circumstances changed.

Theodora of Vasta lived in the tenth century in a small town in Greece. It is said that when bandits attacked her village, she wanted to help defend it. Because she was a woman, it was unthinkable for her to do this, so she disguised herself as a man to protect her people. She was mortally injured, and as she lay there dying, the story is that her last words were, "Let my body become a church, my hair a forest of trees, and my blood a spring to water them."

The villagers, moved by her sacrifice, built a church on the site of her death. From the outside, the tops of the trees can be seen even today, but inside the chapel no evidence of roots or limbs can be found. Scans of the building and the foundation show an underground spring feeding the plant life, which, it appears, grew up through the porous areas inside the walls themselves. The amount of pressure on the building is great, and scientists proclaim it a "miracle" that the building has stood as long as it has. The river that rerouted under the site of the church fed the trees that had sprung up, growing not just around the chapel but also through the walls, supporting the structure even as it disrupted it. The walls become the trees; the trees become the walls, the church becoming the body and the river becoming the blood. The river still being the river, the trees still the trees, the church still the church and yet, also, something else, something more.

I read the story of Theodora and felt it reverberate in me, like a hammer striking the piano string. She was another Mrs. Metaphor, speaking words into the world, crossing over, here on the page. I searched her name, checking each story against the first one I'd found. She shares her name with St. Theodora, wife of Emperor Theophilos, who helped to protect and then restore icons when they were being destroyed in the ninth century; with Theodora, wife of Emperor Justinian, an empress and powerful woman in the sixth century; with Theodora, sister of St. Hermes, who lived in the second century and cared for the sick and imprisoned; and with Theodora of Arta, martyr and miracle-worker.

But Theodora of Vasta shares not only her name but also her feast day with Theodora of Alexandria, a fifth-century saint who, having committed adultery, turned away from her sin and disguised herself as a man in order to enter a monastery and become a monk as penance. She lived a pious life, disguised as a monk, living out her years performing healing and miracles. All of the saints called Theodora were wondrous and strong, miraculous and humble warrior poets, and I wanted to share their name, their qualities, their heritage.

In the Orthodox tradition, we are named, and we are named so that we remember that we are not alone. I'm not the first Angela in my family, not the first Jean, not the first Marie, and not the first Theodora. We take names to remember that people have gone ahead, have smoothed some of the road, and perhaps have torn up other parts. The people who travel before us have left signs to follow, have given instructions on road conditions, on safe places to stop, sights to see, sanctuaries made of walls and trees and rivers flowing, miracles and wonders, body and blood and the bridge in between.

CHAPTER 21

PUTTING IN A GOOD WORD

(on finding a sponsor)

To have faith is like when you trust yourself to the water.
You don't grab hold of the water when you swim.

—Alan Watts

Patient endurance is the fruit of love, for 'love patiently
endures all things' and teaches us to achieve such endur-
ance by forcing ourselves so that through patience we may
attain love.

—St. Gregory Palamas

T he best way to get a job at King's Island was to know someone. The amusement park offered a great hourly salary, fun atmosphere, good food for the employees in the cafeteria, and the prestige of working at a popular summer hangout. I had tried in vain to get my foot in the door, relying on my friend Peg, a past longtime employee, to put in a good word for me. I wanted to work in rides, because that is where the cool people worked. When I did get a call to interview my sophomore year in high school, they offered me a summer position in food service, and I took it, hoping I'd be able to parlay my way into rides as quickly as possible.

In the mornings, Rivertown Potato Works smelled starchy and sterile, but by 10 AM, when we opened, the place was already greasy. By 3 PM, when the heat of the day was at its peak and the floors and countertops showed the residue of our product, the air was pungent with potato skins and fake nacho cheese. The best way to get into rides at King's Island was to know someone, so I pressed Peg to write again to the department head and work toward my transfer. But it never came, and I spent the rest of the summer slinging potatoes and saving money to help pay my high school tuition the following year.

When I returned to King's Island the next summer, I was able to transfer, but only to the pizza place on International Street. No matter how I petitioned, no matter how many times I called, I could not get any closer to rides, so I spent that summer eating leftover LaRosa's pizza every night on my way home from work, grateful to give up smelling like French fries for tomato sauce and mozzarella. Even so, it was another year before I made it to the promised land of the rides department, and the transfer happened because I was tenacious and because of a good word.

FOR A LONG TIME, I ONLY KNEW TWO people who were Orthodox, and they both lived in Missouri. No matter how many books I read and no matter how many churches I visited, I could not get around the basic reality that I was going to have to overcome my issues and make some local friends. If nothing else, it would be necessary for me to meet someone I could ask to usher me into membership. I would need a godparent or a sponsor to vouch for me.

Each time I thought about letting someone get to know me enough so that they could, in good conscience, put in a good word for me, I'd fall into a panic. I constructed at least three emails to my known Orthodox friends who lived several states over, putting out there the possibility that they might stand up for me, and I deleted each one before sending, knowing my motivation each time was some kind of avoidance of the hard stuff.

My social anxiety had slowly built up over years without my even noticing, like calcium deposits in a cave. When I had only been attending Orthodoxy 101 with Father Gregory for about a year, I asked how to move to the next level. I was a regular attendee at Vespers, but I still had not met anyone outside of the other catechumens.

He said that to come to Liturgy was the best way to meet people and find a sponsor. I asked if he could just assign me someone, like in the freshman year of high school when we were assigned a senior "big sister" to guide us into the new territory; but he said he could not. So much for shortcuts.

Our daughter was born while we were in the thick of our

church plant, Metanoia. Riley was our first child and Metanoia our first church startup. We were the first to get married in our group and the first to have a baby. It was a year of firsts. Dave wasn't raised with the tradition of choosing godparents for children, but I wanted that for our baby, and so we introduced the concept to our mixed bag of fellow wanderers. We chose our closest friends to walk alongside for Riley. In choosing, we looked at the people we trusted the most, the people we imagined the kids could turn to with questions of faith and life. We hoped that making that commitment to one another would somehow bind us together with the people who were important in our lives at that time. For each of our subsequent children, we chose in this way. Only a couple of the godparents had any experience with the tradition, and they depended on us to give instruction on what we needed them to do or to be in the life of our children. In truth, we really didn't know what we needed, and we had no one to help us discern that.

Metanoia eventually came to an end, and our small tribe was scattered to the far reaches of Chicago and the suburbs. Everyone was beginning to start families and root themselves in their lives, and without a shared faith community and a shared location, we found our boats all drifting apart, because it's like that in the water. Our friendships remained, as they often do, ready to resume whenever we saw each other, but anchored just a bit further away every time.

When my new friend Nina invited my family to a barbecue at their house on the Fourth of July, I said "maybe" because it was hard to say "yes." I had only known her a short time at St. John Chrysostom, and it went against my normal hermit-like tendencies. For years it was Dave who dragged me out on holidays and business dinners and outdoor concerts to meet new people and to network. I was a terrible date sometimes, especially for the networking parts. He once took me to a late-night "after" party at a film festival so he could meet some high-level producers for a project, and while he worked the room, I sat in the corner nursing one cocktail and chatting with a very nice person who basically worked in the mailroom. It was the most interesting conversation I'd had all night.

When Nina asked me to the barbecue, we'd already met a couple of times through a mutual, albeit non-Orthodox, friend. We had a lot in common—children, homeschooling, our friend Beth, and now Orthodoxy. When I saw her at St. John's, I'd wave a little and walk to the opposite side of the small room, not wanting to insert myself into her space, not wanting to assume.

It was a strange feeling to meet people once I was a catechumen, recognizing I was in need of a godparent. I found myself sizing up every person I met, measuring them for the role I needed filled like an undertaker measuring gunfighters in movies about the Old West. It felt awkward and wrong, and I wondered in every conversation with the new Orthodox people I met if they knew somehow that I had this secret agenda. Though I tried to be nonchalant about it, the thought burned in me every single time. It was hard to be patient and to make the time to build the relationship. I was afraid of choosing poorly, afraid of being turned down, afraid of disappointing, afraid of being disappointed.

The last time I had to choose a sponsor, I was being confirmed in the Catholic Church. Though it came at a time in my life when I probably needed it the most, eighth grade might have been the worst time to ask me to make a choice for mentoring and sponsoring. My parents' relationship was coming apart. What had been fraying at the edges for years was now actively ripping and tearing as they drifted further and further away from each other, anchoring just a bit more apart with each argument, each word, each action. Safe harbors were clouded by the fog of the day, and there were only a few lighthouses to show us the way. In the end I chose Muzzie to be my confirmation sponsor, mainly to balance out the grandmother jealousies that were perpetually fueled by Grandma Doll being my baptismal godparent. I thought it was my job to keep everything balanced and everyone happy.

Presbytera Marion was sitting in a lawn chair by the dormant fire pit in Nina's jungle-like East Nashville backyard. It was blazing hot that July 4, and as my boys ran off to join the water-gun wars in the trees and bushes near the back, I sat down in a chair near the cool, dark fire pit. Nina introduced me to Presbytera, stumbling through at least two names and a title so quickly I was not sure what to call her. I'd seen her at Liturgy and knew she was married to Father Parthenios, but we'd never spoken. She was kind and funny, and the first thing she asked me is if I'd ever heard of "beer margaritas." Her son had just introduced the concept to her, and so that's what we talked about during that first meeting. I knew right away that I liked her.

When I finally worked up the nerve to email her and ask to meet for coffee so that I could get to know her better, I realized I had no idea what name to use in my greeting. I knew she was born Jesse and became Marion, but her role was presbytera—spelled this way for the most part, but also *presvytera* in other places. I opened the email to invite her to coffee with a spam-like but generic, "Hello! We met the other day at Nina's," and that sufficed for the time being. Over the course of several emails and a few coffees, I managed to avoid calling her anything at all, until finally without any prompting she wrote, "Why don't you just refer to me as Presbytera?" and so I did.

The role of presbytera means more than simply being the wife of the priest. The word itself comes from the Greek word for "priest," *presbyteros*, which means literally "elder." When I'd refer to her, to people who did not know her, I'd remember that each time. It was important to me that I introduce her as "Marion, my presbytera," because it was her name and her role, and that was a gift to me.

I took to emailing her with my questions, rants, and confusions. She answered patiently, always telling it to me straight without sugarcoating. She had a long and rich perspective on being a convert, and being the wife of a priest, mother of grown and well-adjusted children, made her a good choice for a conversation partner. The fact that she raised chickens, kept bees, and farmed the small area of land they owned in the middle of the city of Nashville—and that she enjoyed beer margaritas—was just icing on the cake of our friendship.

I moved back to Chicago only a short time after we began our friendship. I was overwhelmed with the transition, finding a new church, meeting new people. Sizing them up for the potential of sponsoring me into the faith was a paralyzing thought. I emailed with Marion a few times about the transition, about the church search, about wearing a head covering, skirts, and combat boots to Liturgy. I talked about rebellion and disappointment and fear, and her responses were always grace and humor in a good mix. She even asked me to send a photo of the combat boot/skirt combo I sported when I was visiting churches so she could get an accurate picture in her head on that.

She was a straight-shooter on theological troubles, a thoughtful conservative on social matters, and a source of support and peace when things were crazy for me, which was always. So when the time was right, I asked her to come to Chicago, put her hand on my shoulder, and lend her "yes" when the time came as my godmother. And thank God, she agreed.

CHAPTER 22

THE MYSTERY OF FAITH

(on confession)

Just as a strongly flowing fountain is not blocked up by a handful of earth, so the compassion of the Creator is not overcome by the wickedness of His creatures.

—St. Isaac of Syria

Confession of errors is like a broom which sweeps away the dirt and leaves the surface brighter and clearer. I feel stronger for confession.

—Mahatma Gandhi

I always thought that because of the phrase, "turning up like a bad penny," at one time there were literally "bad" pennies. People would get the bad penny and put it right back into circulation, and it would wind its way around the neighborhood, the city, the country maybe. It would turn up again and again, and no one would turn it in, no one would throw it away. (In fact, that is true.)

I throw away pennies all the time now. Not because they're bad, but because they mean so little. I vacuum them up along with small toy parts and dust bunnies. Pennies are a kind of colonic for my vacuum cleaner, clearing out the old Cheerios and rabid dust bunnies from the attachment hoses. They don't mean much in a time when no difference is made between one penny and one hundred pennies, and so I throw them away. I may have thrown out some of those bad pennies. How I would know? I barely look at them anymore. Who does?

But now that pennies mean so little, there really aren't any bad pennies. There are just pennies lying around, waiting for some action. Take a penny, leave a penny. Tax rates and inflation nearly promise that we'll never be inclined to take one, but I'll leave one, every single time. At some point in my lifetime, the US government will probably put an end to pennies. They have so little place, it seems. It takes too many of them to make a difference, at least in my comfortable life.

When I was a kid, my best friend Margaret used to tell me that if I found a penny on the ground heads up, it was good luck, but tails up was bad luck. I still believed in luck then, and I took this seriously. Collecting pennies forty years ago was still a viable method of gaining cash, so walking past a tails-up was hard for me; but I left it there. I didn't want any more bad luck. I wanted my dad to get another job and my mom to get good grades at college. I wanted to fit in at school. I wanted my brothers to stop fighting. I wanted to be able to buy a pair of clogs like the ones Margaret had, not the knockoff version from Woolworth but the real ones with the wood soles. They were not practical, and we had no money to spend on impractical shoes.

Pennies on the ground had value to me then: they were penny candy, saving up for something, stock in the future. Passing up the ones found tails-up was a struggle, but I did it. Somewhere along the line, I developed a habit when I ran across tails-side-up pennies. I would turn them over and will myself to walk away. I would turn them heads-up in the hope that the next kid to happen along would find them and have the luck I wanted. I hoped maybe there were other kids out there turning over tails-up pennies on my behalf. I thought this one action, this one small, quiet action, might have some lasting effect on the world at large. I thought in some way I was an instrument of good, a bringer of luck, a participant in the unseen magic that wove us all together. I never told a soul about this habit. Let us proclaim the mystery of faith.

SISTER BASIL WAS PLUMP AND ANCIENT. Shrouded in her long black habit, she taught piano to my older brother and me. I was starting the first grade, and my brother was in the second. Sister Basil did not usually take students before the second grade, but because we were siblings and because I was a girl and she felt girls made more focused students, she made an exception. I waited in one of two chairs facing the piano while my brother took his lesson. He waited in the same chairs while I had mine. The wait was bearable only because the chairs sat just in front of a bookcase, and piled high on the bookcase was the largest stack of comic books I had ever seen. While I waited for my lesson, I would page through *Archie* and *Donald Duck* comics, always wondering how the arthritic nun had managed to amass such a collection. It occurred to me one day that she might have been confiscating them from students for years. The comic I held in my hand to pass the time as I listened to plunking, missteps, and rapping of knuckles perhaps had once belonged to an unlucky student in Sister Basil's high school Latin or algebra classes.

It was the advertising in the back of the comics I liked best. There were ads for X-ray glasses and trick gum, *Grit* magazine, diplomas by mail, and good-luck charms. I needed a good-luck charm, or so I thought. For weeks, I read those ads over and over during my brother's lesson, hoping for that charm, certain it would be just what my family needed to flourish through the disagreements, to survive my dad's job changes and help us navigate the nights my mom spent at school finishing her degree. When my brother's lesson was done one week, I asked Sister Basil if I could borrow the magazine. She waved one wide-knuckled finger in my face and instructed me to return it to the stack the following week.

In my room at home, I took paper and envelope from the stationery set my aunt had given me for my birthday and carefully wrote out the address information. I copied the order form requirements onto the lavender paper rimmed with flowers and kittens, adding my own information. The ad promised luck and fortune. It promised money in the mail; it promised success and achievement. Since money was always tight for us, I was sure this good-luck charm would help.

When it came time to add the money and the stamp, I gathered up the small stash of coins I kept in my top drawer and took it all to my mother. I handed her the envelope, bulging and jingling with order form and coins, and I asked if she had a stamp. It took her a moment to understand what I was doing. She read the order carefully, and I watched as her eyebrows pulled together, deepening the crease that resided there. She knelt down and looked at me.

"We don't believe in this," she said. "We don't buy these things because . . . well, because we're Catholic. We don't believe in good-luck charms." I nodded, because I thought I understood. What I heard her say was that to turn to good-luck charms was against our religion, and I was panicked to think I might have almost done something wrong. I was always afraid of doing something wrong, something against my religion.

THE INCENSE AND THE BELLS DISAPPEARED from the Mass somewhere along the line while I was growing up. I noticed them missing, like a chair I loved at a relative's house that suddenly vanished between visits. It's possible the adults in our parish knew this was coming. I don't remember getting a memo. They were simply there one day and gone the next.

The confessional practices changed, too, over the course of time. My earliest memories of confession were with Father Boyle. From behind the sliding wooden window of the confessional, I would see the side of Father Boyle's face and hear the deep boom of his voice when he spoke, even when he meant to whisper. Sometimes, during the weekly visit to confession, I would get stuck and forget my sins. I would struggle. Once, I made up sins—nothing too outlandish, nothing unbelievable. I just didn't want to come empty-handed, as if bringing my sins to the priest were a kind of hostess gift for a party he threw. He gave me the Body and Blood of Christ twice a week at Mass; the least I could do was to bring my sins into that wooden box.

In the wake of the good-luck charm transgression, I was afraid to go to confession. I was always afraid that at any moment everything would fall apart at home, but at least I was content to know that my salvation, my safe place, my church life was made and rooted in concrete. There was something comforting in that church building, that wooden confessional, in the ritual, in the structure and the predictable nature of the liturgy.

I was afraid to confess that day, but I did it anyway. Father Boyle's labored breathing and heavy sigh came from behind that window in the wooden wall between us. I waited, staring down at my knobby bruised knees and shins. I was always falling, up the stairs because I was running too fast for my ever-lengthening skinny legs, or falling to the sidewalk running to school in shoes too big or too small. I stared at my knees, picking at the scabs, and I waited for Father Boyle to tell me whether my lapse in faith was forgiven. I worried that my wish for a good-luck charm was breaking some long-made canon of the Catholic faith: do not worship another god, do not take the Name in vain, honor thy mother and father. The concrete foundation felt paper-thin and fragile. I felt paper-thin and fragile, but Father Boyle simply spoke words of understanding, of forgiveness, and gave me the usual penance—ten Hail Marys, ten Our Fathers. I knelt there before the candle stand in front of the Mother of God, and I prayed fervently, because I still felt I had failed and I could not let it go.

When I was in middle school, finally the wooden confessional boxes were discarded in favor of "face-to-face" confession. Perhaps the authorities felt the boxes were useless and outdated; perhaps the church was trying to be forward-thinking and modern. The confessionals were moved to the basement, and they sat in the corners of the all-purpose room, unused, forgotten.

Instead, we sat in chairs, Father Boyle shifting uncomfortably; his girth and cassock disagreed with the metal chairs designed as a stand-in for the confessional. I shifted uncomfortably; my sins and shame disagreed with the idea that Father Boyle would see my face as I spoke them. I blushed. Probably everyone blushed. Perhaps Father Boyle was blushing. I looked at the floor the whole time. I did not want to be seen. I only wanted to be heard and then forgiven so that I could move to the candle stand before the statue of the Mother of God and say my penance prayers.

The mystery of the moment was lost when the wooden confessionals were retired, when the incense was put away, when the bells were removed. Mass had always been an otherworldly experience, one I could not wait to encounter, and then suddenly it was stripped bare, like candlelight replaced by fluorescent bulbs.

FATHER JOHN SUGGESTED I MAKE A LIST for my confession before my chrismation into the Orthodox faith. He said people often forgot in the moment what they wanted to say. I knew I would not forget. Confession has become more than a hostess gift for the priest now that I have rounded the second base of my forties. I find I am more likely to pry up the lid on sin than to tuck it into a closet. I know my pitfalls. I know my tendencies. It is those that disturb me most.

It's not the swear words that escape my lips when I'm driving with the kids in the car; it is the lack of remorse that follows. It's not the loss of my temper around dinnertime every day; it is the justification and entitlement I feel because I had a hard day. It's not the drifting thoughts and judgmental attitudes; it is the apathy that comes when I'm faced with repentance. It is when I am afraid to change, afraid to try, afraid that if I give up the verbal slips, the angry outbursts, and the judgmental attitudes there will only be a gaping hole in me. It is when I am afraid to give up the sin and the doubt and the fear because I do not know what will come to reside in that gaping hole. It is when I begin to think I love the sin more than the redemption. Sin is familiar. Redemption is a gamble. It's fear that keeps me here.

So I confessed this. I confessed my inability to right myself when I'm tilting. I confessed my defiance and my anger. I confessed my doubt and my lacking and my apathy. And I confessed that more than likely, future confessions would simply be another version of this one. I worry that maybe I'm too old to change now, too set in my ways to embrace the real essence of confession the way I did when I was young.

The turning away from sin is a 180-degree maneuver. Not only must I be willing to turn my back on the old behavior and attitude; I'm required to lean into the new. If I truly repent of my angry outbursts, it means giving up that desperate grab at control. It means I unclench my fists and open my palms, facing up, waiting and expectant, knowing full well they may stand empty for a while. I may fold those hands back in on themselves time after time in anger and frustration and fear. But repentance means that after each confession, I embrace the soft hands, I embrace the open posture, the vulnerable, the unfilled, the gaping space waiting. It's a gamble.

The government may get rid of pennies now, finding them useless and outdated. They may gather them up and melt them down. Perhaps they'll become a commodity, a collector's dream. But there are no bad pennies any more, and maybe there are no lucky pennies or unlucky pennies either. There is only the habit we develop—to overcome our fears and doubts—of picking up those pennies or leaving them, or turning them over with the intention of paying it forward. The intention is the thing, the hope that some good could come in the wake of this small action. There is only tradition and history and moving forward into the future while feeling the weight of that penny in my pocket, or lifted from my shoulders as a reminder, somehow, of things lost and things found. Let us proclaim the mystery of faith.

CHAPTER 23

Beginning Clean

(on fasting and failing)

Let the mouth also fast from disgraceful speeches and railings. For what does it profit if we abstain from fish and fowl and yet bite and devour our brothers and sisters? The evil speaker eats the flesh of his brother and bites the body of his neighbor.

—St. John Chrysostom

The Lenten journey is not about what you cannot eat. It's about what you pray from your heart while fasting and God daily feeding your spirit.

—Subdeacon Michael Chuck Hann

On the top shelf in our walk-in pantry, behind the melba toast and the cans of tuna my mother used to eat while dieting, behind the cereals we did not like, behind the tin of rum balls that had lived in that pantry longer than we had lived in that house, there were a few bottles of soda pop called Tahitian Treat. We knew they were there, though they were hidden. They were only for my mother's consumption. None of us kids would even consider breaking the sacred trust of the forbidden pantry shelf by violating the bottles of bright red fizzy sugar water.

My mother always seemed to be dieting. When things were particularly stressful in the household, we'd find remnants of junk food, wrappers and crumbs, perhaps an empty bottle of Tahitian Treat, near the floor register where she would sit late at night and study for her college classes. A few days after that, the pantry would once again be filled with melba toast and canned tuna fish—remorse for the sins of the past, recommitment to the true path of a smaller dress size.

In the Orthodox tradition, we fast. A lot. No matter how many calendars I printed and pasted on my refrigerator door, remembering the weekly fast was a struggle. I would forget halfway through each Wednesday and Friday and find myself eating meat or dairy without thinking. I'd clunk myself on the forehead in "I should have had a V8" style and finish out the day limping along across the fasting finish line with all kinds of remorse.

When I began the journey into Orthodoxy, I was already moving again toward becoming a vegetarian, with designs on moving on to being a full-on casual vegan. I thought this part of the practice would be the easiest to wrap my hands around.

After spending most of my life having people compliment me on my trim waistline, I noticed I was beginning to expand my physical horizons, and I thought changing my diet might help. It wasn't just the weight gain that moved me toward the vegetarian lifestyle, but aging in general, the fatigue, the need for more coffee in the mornings and sometimes in the middle of the day, and the fact that I had already tried so many other diets to stem my growing pants size.

I tried the low-carb and the high-vegetable and the juicing and the whole grains and the no grains and the grapefruit and the cottage cheese and pineapple, finding myself understanding my mother more and more with each switch. While I blamed perimenopause, natural aging, or low thyroid function and chronic fatigue syndrome for the weight gain, it was more likely that my expanding form was a result of the eating I did in secret, the hidden treats, the sneak snacking, medicating the emotional ills by feeding them sugar and trans fats.

By the time we moved on to the Presbyterian church, I'd lost the secret nature of the eating and moved on to utter defiance, choosing the chocolate-covered donut in the church potluck lineup because "so what" and "who cares" and "mind your own business." My body frame supported this gain, so while it was easy to hide, I knew it was a lie when I looked in the mirror after getting out of the shower. I told myself I was fat and sighed with disgust when I looked in the mirror, and that did more damage to me than the junk food ever could.

Orthodox Christians fast twice a week in ordinary time,

abstaining from meat and dairy and sometimes wine and olive oil. We also enter into several longer fasts throughout the year, most notably, becoming vegan for forty days during the season of Lent. I struggled through the fast days, Lent, the Apostles' fast, and the fast of the Dormition of the Theotokos that first year, thinking if only I could have more time, more energy, or a personal chef, I would finally be able to keep it all together long enough to avoid the burgers and milkshakes I was craving.

I relished the idea of forty days in the early spring each year to clean out my system and make room for something new, something redeeming. I thought it might compensate for all the moments I was inclined to forgo my pseudo-healthy lifestyle and toss that Butterfinger on the belt at the grocery store, hidden under the kale and the bulgur wheat. When the clerk scanned it, I'd snatch it up immediately and hide it in my purse. I'd eat it quickly in the drive from the store to the house, removing all evidence before entering the sacred kitchen where I espoused whole foods and demonized sugar to my children.

REMEMBER YOU ARE DUST. AS CATHOLICS, we would start the season of Lent with Ash Wednesday. At St. Teresa of Avila grade school, we would file into the cold church for Mass, as we did every Wednesday. At the appointed time we'd shuffle forward to receive the ashes on our forehead, Father Boyle's fat thumb making the sign of the cross under our bangs. The closer you were to the start of the line, the better chance you'd have that the smudge would resemble the sign of the Cross. The unwritten and unspoken rule was to wear those ashes throughout the day, so we would sit at dinner with our fish sticks and tartar sauce, watching reruns of Star Trek, and have no conversation about the black smudges we all sported.

No matter which church denomination I was dating at the time, I would always find a way to receive ashes at the start of Lent. I would leave the ashes on my forehead during my work day or my college classes as some kind of outward sign, perhaps a strange sideways rebellion against the secular nature of the life I was constructing, or more likely, an instinctual lean toward the familiar rhythm of things I'd always known—I was made of dust, and to dust I would return. Receiving ashes connected me to my home, to the faith of my family and my friends growing up. Receiving ashes connected me to the body, to the transient flesh. It went hand in hand with sacrifice and widespread "fasting" from things, behaviors, attitudes.

I gave up candy every year when I was a child; I then made myself sick on Easter Sunday by gorging on the very thing I'd laid aside for forty days. When I was older, I "gave up" television or fighting with my brothers or complaining about going to school, failing day after day, but keenly aware of my limitations nonetheless. By the time Easter arrived, more often than not the sacrifice had petered out, and I was back to every attitude, every behavior, every eating habit I'd been avoiding. It would be another year until the ashes would grace my head again, another year before I would shuffle forward and hear the reminder about being ash, being born of fire, fueled by oil, redeemed by water.

Recently, after a long holiday weekend, Dave took his blood pressure. It was too high. He'd been able to finally let go of the beta blocker a couple of years after his heart attack but took out the familiar cuff often to check his blood pressure. The weekend was filled with overindulgence in food and drink and stress. The blood-pressure cuff showed the results of those indulgences. We agreed that on Monday we'd make some adjustments. On Monday, we were beginning clean again, not out of remorse for past deeds or because he wanted to look a certain way, but because his life depended on it.

It occurred to me that we cannot help but choose badly from time to time. The act of beginning clean isn't about shame but about nourishment, treating our bodies not as machines to be tinkered with but as gardens, waiting for care, waiting for water. It wasn't until I became certified as a personal trainer that I stopped understanding my body as a machine and began to know it as a garden. Machines are impersonal, mechanical, and cold. Machines can be separated from me. If my body were a car, I could trade it in when things began to rust. I could upgrade to the latest model. It would not matter how I treated it, how I spoke to it, how I fueled it, because my body would only have value inasmuch as it got me from point A to point B.

I was on a beach in California, on a film shoot with Dave, the day I decided to become a personal trainer. We were newly married. I had picked up some magazines to pass the time for the long flight home. I sat on the beach as Dave waded into the water, and I flipped through the pages of the fitness magazine:

spot reduction, thinner thighs, fighting off sugar highs, exercise for the non-exercise-inclined. But every picture was of a thin, super-fit woman photographed to appeal, to be the standard for us. This is the woman I was supposed to want to be—happy, active, athletic. The fitness magazine made it seem so simple, offering the panacea for health and happiness, three-point systems to get perfect arms and flat abs.

It was all within reach in these pages, and I was angry there on the beach, because it was such a terrible lie. I was not a machine with defective parts to be replaced, and I knew in that moment that I was not alone in thinking this. I was not alone in muttering to myself about my fat thighs and ugly skin. I realized if I spoke to a child the way I spoke to myself about my body, it would be considered downright abusive, and I could not let that stand. So I ordered the books, took the necessary courses, and passed the exam.

As Catholics, we would never say "alleluia" during Lent, because it was joyful and we were in mourning. It seemed the purpose of the forty days was lament, shame, grief, and punishment. We sacrificed because Christ sacrificed. We gave things up because Christ gave Himself up. It was the least we could do. Whether it fit the canon of the Catholic Church or not, this was the understanding I came to about Lent, and for years after that I only knew Lent to be a time of anguish, preparing myself for Jesus being nailed to a tree on my behalf. It was a heavy load.

Even so, when Lent rolled around that first year of my conversion, I missed the feel of the ash on my forehead. When I lamented this, my Orthodox friend Scott said, "But we have Clean Monday, and that's even better."

In the Orthodox tradition, Lent begins with Clean Monday. We spend the two Sundays previous cleaning out the pantry and the refrigerator of the foods we'll be putting aside for forty days. Meatfare Sunday and Cheesefare Sunday often find church communities sharing in what is left, offering up a feast. It is celebratory and strange yet beautiful and bonding.

The day following Cheesefare Sunday is called Clean Monday. We start here—open, fortified, and willing, like soil tilled and ready for seed. Clean Monday isn't about reminding me that I am dust as much as it is about reminding me that I am a garden, deserving of care, deserving of redemption. Rather than plunging ourselves into the absence of "alleluia," the Orthodox make room for it, because though the reminder that we are dust is a good one, the reminder that we are redeemed is a better one in the forty days leading up to Pascha.

I spent most of my life reducing myself to dust, comparing myself against other women, other mothers, other Christians, and pounding myself into some contrived and sacrificial image of a cog in a great machine. But I am a garden, not a machine. Beginning clean means making space for the good things, emptying out a year's worth of abuse and neglect, pulling the weeds and trimming the overgrown branches. It is renewal and it is life, and it is not without struggle, because gardening is hard work. Growing things need care.

CHAPTER 24

THE FAIRER SEX

(on being a modern woman in an ancient tradition)

We all fight over what the label "feminism" means but for me it's about empowerment. It's not about being more powerful than men —it's about having equal rights with protection, support, justice. It's about very basic things. It's not a badge like a fashion item.

—Annie Lennox

Whenever I visualize my options in the Mary vs. Martha debate, I'm always Mary, never Martha. I'm sitting in the room with the men, at the feet of Jesus, while Martha makes magic of her own in the other room. She curses me under her breath, not because she could use my help, but because we're so different, and because she believes her way is the right way, just as I believe my way, though unorthodox, is right too. We are two halves of one complete, perfect force of nature, powerful and compelling and at odds all the time.

My daughter was outraged and disgusted as she told me the story of her camping trip with her grandma to Idaho. She was outraged and disgusted that Grandma would let the boys her age ride the trails on their own but would not allow Riley the same freedom. I let her rail on about it for a long time, conflicted myself about what to say and what not to say. Discernment didn't come easily, because I wanted her to be protected, and because I knew also how unfair it was to be treated differently based solely on our biology.

The reality struck me when I was her age as well, that we, as women, could be invaded so easily, that we were a target because we were women, and I was afraid. My daughter chooses to be angry about that historical reality. Her anger and her energy around it are encouraging to me. She has some clarity I did not have in that moment, perhaps, some courage or context I might have had once but lost when I had a daughter of my own. As with most things, it's different from the inside. Parenting looks a certain way before the babies arrive. It's easy to judge, easy to plan, easy to consider what kind of upbringing we'll encourage, what kind of safety net we'll build.

At ten years old, patriarch-heavy doctrine, history, and tradition made little sense to me. It all seemed aimed at keeping girls at a distance, keeping our hands away from the moving pieces of the Mass. So I arranged a meeting to discuss the issues I was having. I met with Father Boyle, Sister Martha Mary, Herb Huebner the choir director, and two of my female classmates in a small office in the rectory. I had taken some initiative and formed an equality committee of sorts one day on the playground after Mass. We did not understand why we could not be altar servers and why there was a boys' choir but not a girls' choir, why we were excluded, unseen, and unheard.

We presented our case to Father Boyle with our clearest arguments for equality. We only wanted a chance. The choir director was not opposed to forming a girls' choir, and because it broke no doctrinal rules, it was the only demand Father Boyle could meet from our self-made equality committee. He might have explained tradition and doctrine and dogma regarding girls as altar servers, but I don't remember that part. I remember only that we were given the girls' choir that day, that we could leave class early once a week to rehearse, and that we would sing on Wednesdays at Mass once a month and on Sundays for special occasions. We took our small victory, and we were content for a little while, because we had to start somewhere.

In those days, the Sisters of Mercy still wore the familiar long black habits at St. Teresa of Avila grade school. Only the newer, younger sisters had taken the Vatican II suggestions to heart, opting for modern skirts, button-down light blue shirts, and sensible shoes, while keeping the headgear and traditional cross pendant in place. While it was easy to spot a nun even in their "civvies," some of the older population of Catholics at our parish took issue with the modern ways of the newcomers. By the time I reached high school, some of the sisters stopped wearing the headgear as well, showing off short, simple, uniform haircuts as the identifier of their calling as the Bride of Christ.

Sister Basil was one of the last to still sport the flowing black robes at my high school. She was stern and ancient, still teaching Latin to freshmen into her eighties. I took the class because I remembered her teaching me piano when I was young, and because I loved the origin of words and wanted to know more. When I reminded Sister Basil in class that first week that she had once taught my piano lessons, she pretended to remember, but I could see that she did not. I was the awkward girl with an awkward, unshared memory with an eighty-year-old nun, and I let it hang there in the classroom like that until we opened our books to read aloud the Introduction to Latin. Within a few weeks, Sister Basil became ill. She never came back to class, a young Sister of Mercy taking her place. Sister Basil died a little before the end of my freshman year.

FOR TEN YEARS AS AN ADULT, I PRAYED for a mentor. I prayed because my friend Paula suggested it when we were in Metanoia, and because I had no idea what it would look like to have a mentor, in particular a female mentor. Paula and I identified each other early in our friendship as soul sisters, and though we both loved and valued the guidance of our mothers, we lamented the absence of mentors outside of that. We wished for them, and we talked in as much detail as possible about what those female mentors might look like, sound like, dress like.

As I prayed for her day after day and year after year, I formed an image, and usually she looked like a Sister of Mercy— sometimes in full habit, sometimes in layman's dress. She was confident and she was wise. She had good thoughts on difficult questions. She was not imposing, and she was not shaming. For ten years, each time I met a woman who might fit the bill I would size her up, I would test her, and I would pray, and each time I would turn away, thinking my list was still unfulfilled.

When I met Mary Earle at Laity Lodge the year I became a catechumen, I was nervous and I did not know why. An old familiar joke came to me in that moment about a man who is stranded on top of a house in a flood. Surrounded by rising waters, he prays for God to save him. A boat comes by and offers a ride, but the man refuses, saying he believes God will save him. A few hours later, a larger boat comes by and offers assistance, but the man refuses, again saying he thinks God will save him. Finally, a helicopter comes and drops a line, but the man refuses, saying God will save him. When the man dies, he greets God in heaven, and he is angry. "Why didn't You save me?" he shouts. God lifts his hands. "I sent two boats and a helicopter. What more did you need?"

The afternoon I returned home, I emailed Mary E to ask if she would mentor me. For ten years I prayed for a mentor, and for ten years God was faithful, bringing amazing women across my path, and I turned away each one in favor of some kind of fantasy that there might be one person who was perfect, who could guide me with God's very hand. I admit, I was too arrogant to see how my deep need meant that I could use all the help He could send.

The "Woman Within" was a sort of emotional and spiritual Outward Bound weekend, counterpart to a men's weekend my husband had done before we met. It was meant as a kind of initiation into womanhood, and I jumped in not knowing what to expect. The question asked of me the first night rang in my ears: "I know I am a woman because . . ."

I was in a large room far from my loft apartment and far from my husband. I had persuaded my friend Dawn to come with me because I did not want to be alone. The spiritual component to the weekend was meant to embrace all faiths, all viewpoints. It was cobbled together with Sufi songs and Rumi poetry, with Native American symbolism and Christian morality plays. It was part therapy and part exploration, and for the weekend, it seemed to work somehow.

We stood in that big room, one circle of women facing out and another circle of women standing opposite us, unknown faces, all nervous, all afraid, all ready and willing to answer the questions put before us. "I know I am a woman because . . ." was answered by some with biological answers, one woman next to me cupping her ample bosom and laughing. "These!" she said, a little too loudly, and we laughed.

But I was stuck. It was more than biological, more than personality, more than emotional. I did not know how to answer. I saw myself then in Sister Mary Martha's classroom on a hot day, jealous that my body was still stick-like while my friend Colleen was rounding out in the best places. I thought of my first date and my first kiss. I grasped for that one moment when at last I understood that I was no longer a girl, that I was a woman. I struggled with the realization that I had no idea what it meant to be a woman at all. I shrugged to my partner and admitted as much. "I just don't know."

From the moment I met Mary Earle at the poetry workshop in 2010, I liked her. My hair was a nearly flame-red orange that weekend, a result of miscommunication with a new hairdresser mixed with a midlife crisis. When Dave saw the cut and color, he was taken aback, but he smiled and told me he liked it. I liked it too, and so I kept it.

Mary sat across from me at dinner the first day of the workshop; she was confident and kind, older than I, talkative and inquisitive. I listened to the conversation she began with the people at our table, and she turned to ask me about my life. I spoke a little about myself, embarrassed, still unable to respond to that common question "What do you do?" with any winning answer. So I hemmed and hawed a little and then made a joke.

She said she'd enjoyed my thoughts in our workshop that day, and then she leaned forward to say that when she saw me for the first time, she knew she liked my spirit. She said she told her husband at that moment, "She has *chispa!*" and she smiled, adding, "It's Spanish. It means spark." When I told Mary I was exploring Orthodoxy, she was only a little bit surprised. She said she, too, had flirted with it, but because she wanted to be a priest, she could never commit to it. She gave me suggestions of books to read, and she said she would pray for me and answer any questions that were within her reach.

We traded poems, and I wondered why it didn't bother me that becoming Orthodox meant I could not be a priest. After all my rants about equality and freedom and rights, when faced with joining a tradition that would not ordain women into the priesthood, I felt strangely at home with it. After all the years I'd argued with Father Dennis in religion class and petitioned with Father Boyle about girls as altar servers, I was oddly at home in a tradition that offered no path to priesthood for women. It bothered me that I was not more resistant to the idea.

THE WISE WOMAN BUILDS HER HOUSE. IN the great room, standing in front of the river rock fireplace, I read poetry and scripture, hands raised at one time or another, fingertips pressed together to accent this passage, that word, a breath, a moment, a pause. The faces of the women before me are eager and afraid. They don't know what to expect, because we've kept that hidden. They were the third or fourth group to come through this experience I'd put together over years of coffee dates and emails and books shared among my friends and myself.

Some of the women who sat with me staffing the weekend we called "The Wise Woman" had known me for ten, fifteen, or twenty years. We all grieved the missing piece in our lives, and we all wanted it for the women we met, the daughters we loved, the sisters we lay-counseled in parking lots and grocery stores. We started with the same circle I'd encountered years before at the Woman Within, asking some of the same questions about becoming a woman, about knowing, about not knowing. The brave women who came through each weekend were trusting, the air was heavy with shame and doubt and fear and anger, and we all swam through it together to keep from drowning. In the Great Room on the last day of each weekend, Sunday morning, we held our own version of worship, shifting the focus from our own pain to give thanks, to break bread, to offer the cup, and to participate in our own brand of Liturgy.

When the smoke cleared after each of these weekends, I would find myself in pieces on the floor. While driving, even days later, I would have to pull over and break down on my steering wheel. It took weeks sometimes to put myself back together and hold it all close. It took work to keep the secrets I'd heard. It took an astonishing amount of effort to be in that holy place, given such responsibility, time after time, untethered, unrooted, unprepared. The work was good and necessary, and I had a natural inclination for leading it, but it was tearing me apart.

I wrote to Mary E to ask her advice, because she had a great deal of experience with leading retreats and with counseling. As a priest, she had been trained to be able to handle the confession and the absolution, the leading and the listening. I asked for her prayers and for her insights on how I could do it better.

When I first began to ask Mary for her mentoring, I told her

I expected she would always speak her mind. It was important to me that she pull no punches and be as direct as possible. Mary instructed me, first, to pay attention to the exhaustion and see what it had to say to me, and to pay attention to the answers it gave. She said the Desert Fathers believed exhaustion is a dangerous spiritual state and that it was important I re-evaluate my roles to address it.

I thought about that exhaustion—about my roles as leader, as mother, as writer, as wife. I asked myself what the exhaustion said about these things and about the structure of the weekend, the responsibilities that came with it, the amount of space needed to be able to care for people in this way, with such intensity and such commitment. I was tired already when it all began, and when I looked around my life in the wake of those weekends, I realized that my body, my energy, and my family were bearing the brunt of it all. I was not standing in the grove of trees behind my yard as a child, celebrating the Mass, uncommitted, unconcerned.

In the midst of the journey, I realized that the Wise Woman was not my priesthood, and in that moment even my inner punk rocker, the one who never wanted to be a mother at all, realized that the Wise Woman was not my first responsibility. I had to build my house. I already had a responsibility to the brood of chaos-makers I'd helped to bring into the world and to the person with whom I planned to grow old, and those people were suffering in the wake of that ministerial storm each time. It was not the work or the program or the design. It was the timing.

With all kinds of remorse, I looked down at the work I'd started that was crushed into my tight fist and began to pry open my fingertips to let it go. Over time, I left the program in good hands, with wise women who were trustworthy and true. They were gracious about my leaving and grateful that we'd begun it at all. It was a sacrifice, but it preserved me, and though at times I had fleeting thoughts that I was giving up, it preserved my family, it preserved my house. I realized in that moment that my priesthood at this point in my life was the family I had in front of me.

When my daughter questions me on how I can enter into a tradition so steeped in what she reads as a patriarch's heavy boot on a modern woman's neck, I pause and consider it. I have no clear and easy answer for this. I anticipate that with time and discussion and prayer, I will begin to understand more the greater, wider, deeper aspects of Orthodoxy as it pertains to being a woman. I anticipate that I will wrestle with this, that I will engage it, that I will reason with it, until at some point— perhaps many years in the future—I will have an answer for her that makes sense.

All I know is that at this moment, on the brink of becoming Orthodox, I do believe that it's different on the inside. On the inside, it is my difficulty to engage, it is my giant to wrestle, it is my discussion group. I can tell her that for now, I know I can enter into Orthodoxy because the quest to be ordained or to expand the role of women in the church or in the world or in politics will always have its importance to me. I won't stop caring about those issues. Standing on the outside of parenting, it felt as though I could do it all and do it well, but it was different from the inside. I could not possibly know from the outside how to engage that task.

For myself, at this moment, the question is more personal, more intimate. The roaring from the tall grass ahead warns that I will lose something, some freedom or power. The roaring from the tall grass ahead reignites the fear of being reduced or maligned because of my biology, but to run into the roar means that where women's issues are concerned, I can trust in the unfolding of time on this. I can trust that the conversations about equality and about ordination and about the role of women in the church will always be happening, and I can walk alongside in that, entering in when the time is right. I hope it is enough.

It is only now, after twenty years of living with that question asked of me so long ago, that I can begin to answer it. How do I know I am a woman? I know I am a woman because I'm more than ladies' coffees and uncomfortable undergarments. I know I am a woman because I'm more than politics and positioning. I know I am a woman because of my biology and my strength, because of my compassion and mothering, because of my struggle and my peace, because of the house that I build and nurture and bless. I know I am a woman because I am Mary and Martha, Joan and Theodora, Orthodox and Catholic, strong and sensitive, life-giver, soul sister, wise woman, beloved of God.

CHAPTER 25

RUBBER ROOM

(on having a safe place)

*I don't think I need a rubber room, but that might
be nice.*

—Barenaked Ladies

I was sixteen. My parents' divorce was being hashed out, and it was already a year since the proceedings had begun, my mom filing the motion, my dad fighting it. The first year, my dad lived in our basement. He had moved a bed downstairs near the hole he'd carved out in the foundation of the house a few years earlier. His intention in carving out that hole was to make a doggie door, but instead of installing it in the door itself, he used a sledgehammer to make a hole in the concrete wall of the foundation. It took him all day to make the hole large enough for that Irish setter to squeeze out.

When my mom came home, she was livid. They spoke about it in barbed-wire voices. My brothers defended my dad, my sister and I retreated to our room, and the hole in the basement wall remained. To answer my mother's concerns about the heat escaping the basement, my dad installed a carpet-swatch flap on the outside wall. It took some coaxing to get the dog to exit the house through the door, but eventually he went. The trouble was, Prince could leave the basement, but because of the placement of the carpet, he could not get back in. The doggie door never caught on with Prince.

The hole remained there a long time, a constant reminder of missing pieces, hacked-out mortar in the foundation of us. My dad's projects were always like this, whole hog but half considered. Argument and defense and then retreating always followed these intense bursts of inspiration. I knew he meant well. It was misplaced energy at best from a man who had no idea what to do at home.

WHENEVER MY FRIENDS AND I WENT TO the punk hangout in Newport called the Jockey Club, I always drove. I was the only one with my driver's license at sixteen, and our yellow VW bus could fit all of us easily. The Jockey Club was across the river in Kentucky. It was the only punk club we could get into without fake IDs. I got lost every time I drove there, even though it was a simple hop across the bridge. I was afraid of that bridge, of that crossing, and of getting caught doing something I should not be doing.

In retrospect, I can see I was a terrible punk rocker. I defied authority from the safety of the record player. I made my rebellion in deeply personal and perhaps barely distinguishable acts. The trips to the Jockey Club were a minor act. I was not defiant and angry on the bridge to the club. I was terrified. Once there, I stuck to the walls, only entering into the violent dances from the edges, where injury was least likely to show on my arms and legs. I'd light a cigarette, looking tough, waiting for the chance to sneer at someone; but everyone was sneering here. It was easy to blend in, easy to find a place, being the least angry, the least defiant.

The punk clubs of the early eighties, my teenage years, were strange gatherings of people in between. Unlike the seventies, where rebellion was rampant and necessary, the eighties found us caught up in the commercialism and bright colors of pop music. Punk rock was neo-punk at this point, waiting to give birth to the New Wave, to the deep waters of the Alternative music movement I'd discover in college. Punk rock was the old man in the corner at the Jockey Club who checked our IDs, knowing full well the world was changing again and not caring all that much. There would always be a place for punk rock, there along the walls, the edges, the violent slam dance and stage dive. The room was chaos inside, but it was a safe place for rebellion and anger, for working out our salvation from the difficulties of life.

AT A WRITING CONFERENCE A YEAR OR SO
into my time as a catechumen, I ran into a politically liberal
Christian friend at a conference and introduced him to someone. I jokingly called him a sort of heretic where religion was
concerned. His seriousness took me aback. "I'm not a heretic."
It struck me that for so long I used the word heretic when what I
really meant to describe was a free thinker. I'd somehow equated
being liberal or open-minded with being a heretic.

In the religious tradition, the word *heretic* has a distinct
meaning. It is not taken lightly. The word stems from the Greek
meaning "to take" or "to choose." As the word came further
into use, it was meant to denote making a choice apart from
the Catholic or Orthodox Church teaching. To choose a her-
esy meant that someone was turning away from the traditional
teachings of the Church.

This is what went through my head when Father John and I
went over the prayers for chrismation. He ran through the parts
about denouncing my previous heresies, the turning away, the
turning toward. For three years I'd been focused on finding the
connections between where I'd been as a native Catholic, then
later during my tour of Protestantism, and finally where I was
aiming to go, never thinking I would be asked to leave anything
behind. I thought about my mom attending my chrismation and
hearing me call the Catholic beliefs that she still practiced with
great devotion "heresies." I felt I was standing in her basement,
sledgehammer in hand, making holes in the foundation of her
house. It stopped me in my tracks.

It was the unchanging nature of Orthodoxy that drew me in from the start, the structure being solid, built on something deeper than the layer of sand and dirt, built to weather the shifting of cultural things. I wanted that solidity, that history. It was exotic as it stood apart from the churches trying too hard to be coffee shops in the never-ending pursuit of being relevant to someone, to everyone. The foundation of this tradition was thick concrete, a protection from the driving rain and rising waters. It felt safe for me to be able to bounce around. I had thought Orthodoxy might be a giant rubber room, holding me safe while I screamed into the night all my fears and my doubts and my hardships. The rubber room meant my arms could fly, my legs were free, my voice was clear. Knowing my own boundaries felt more empowering than restrictive, more uplifting than oppressive, and yet there was still something in it that didn't sit well with me.

My liberal Orthodox friends would often remind me, when I questioned their ability to go along with the conservative teachings of the Church, that as with most things—like parenting or houses—it's different on the inside. I did realize I was still standing across the street, looking at it from a distance, trying to discern it through the mass of traffic. The border between where I stood from the outside and where I wanted to be seemed thick and uncrossable.

WHEN I WAS A KID, WE COULD RIDE OUR bikes anywhere in the immediate neighborhood—down

Loretta, across Omena and Olivia Lane, up to but not including Rapid Run and Overlook Avenues. Those were busy streets, unpredictable and downright dangerous. We knew the boundaries were there to keep us safe until we knew enough to cross into the larger world, to ride alongside the traffic and make our way out of the familiar and into the unknown without dying in the effort.

The streets became worn into our social system, and rather than resent the boundaries, we laid claim to them. We wanted the safety as much as we reached for exploration. We could sit in the Wenzes' backyard and look through the trees to the promise of adventure. From the high point in our little kingdom, we could see the traffic on Glenway Avenue, we could hear the rush of cars and the busy of the world. Our streets were hilly and meandered, making them a bad choice of short cut between the heavy traffic areas. If a car came down Omena, it was usually going somewhere in our neighborhood, or the people were lost.

We were the monarchs of our kingdom except on Highridge; there were teenagers on Highridge. There, we were minions. By the time we developed neighborhood wanderlust, we were old enough to act on it, old enough to wander out past the corner of Glenway and Overlook, out into Westwood, down to Western Hills, Colerain, and Delhi, where the teenage monarchs went when the kingdom was not enough.

Eventually, the kingdom would not be enough. The boundaries were only there to guide us for a while. They were never meant to be the end of our experience with the world. The

kingdom would always lie just over the next hill, across Overlook and past Highridge and Loretta.

WHEN FACED WITH SCHEDULING, FINALLY,
my chrismation, I called my mom to prepare her. I warned her
on the phone one day that it was possible that while becoming
Orthodox, during the chrismation itself, I would be required to
renounce my "former heresies." I do that. I lay groundwork,
prepare people, and try to smooth the road. Being prepared,
in my estimation, is a way to ease us through the rough spots.
There are boulders ahead; wear sturdy shoes. There are bears
in the woods; bring a knife. There's a chance of rain; bring an
umbrella. It's what responsible people do, or at least it is what I
thought I was supposed to do.

I did not realize how far I'd taken the being-prepared model,
how badly I'd abused it, until one night when talking with my
husband about how I anticipated my daughter might react to a
trip he was planning. I cautioned that she would probably be
upset, reluctant, and maybe even whine about it. I instructed
him to be patient and try to see it her way. Their personality
clashes often centered on his extrovert impulses conflicting with
her introverted tendencies.

He looked at me and shook his head. "Why do you do
that?" he asked calmly. "You plan for disaster," he said, and I
knew he was right. I plan for the worst case, I expect confron-
tation, I prepare for calamity, because if I have the right tools in
my backpack, maybe somehow it will spare me from pain, from

disappointment, from death. I cannot stick to Loretta Avenue anymore, and so I build a virtual tank to take me around the neighborhood, because life is dangerous and I am afraid of that venturing.

When I warned my mom that I would need to renounce "my previous heresies" with the Catholic faith, she sighed on the other end of the phone and said, "Well, you're still allowed to at least socialize with heretics, aren't you?" Then to make sure I knew the question was rhetorical, she followed the statement with a hearty laugh before I could form an answer.

I went into the conversation thinking I was defusing a potentially dangerous conflict. I thought my mother might feel offended or upset or maligned, like the day my dad tore the hole in the wall of our house. It was her house; she had a right to be upset. Thankfully, she is wiser than I am, and she knows I don't live in her house anymore. Becoming Orthodox would not take a sledgehammer to anyone's foundation, including my own. Becoming Orthodox would be filling in those low spots, those holes torn apart already, those places where the rain came in and flooded me when the storm raged outside.

I always joke that the best way to protect my children from the effects of the world, from the traffic, the noise, the confusion, and the constant assault on their innocence, would be for me to bubble-wrap them and place them in a rubber room somewhere. I'd just let them bounce around as much as they could for as long as they'd like, living in that safe, protected place. It's possible an argument against this approach is that they'd be too insulated, too overwhelmed when life finally did break through. It's possible they'd be unprepared for the realities life would offer, the barbed-wire comments, the poisoned imagery, the oncoming cars.

But it's not a terribly good argument for people who have some common sense, really. At a certain point in our development, we don't have to get hit by the oncoming car to understand that it would hurt. We don't have to stand in traffic and test out that theory in order to learn to avoid it. The rush of the car, the wind in our faces, the sound of the engine as it roars around the unseen curve of Overlook Avenue tells us easily at a certain age that at least some marginal safety depends on how we behave when facing the road.

When I embarked on the road to Orthodoxy, I thought it would be that rubber room, that safe house, that predictable shelter from the storm. I thought the practice, the faith, the tradition would all serve as an unchanging home base in an ever-changing playing field. I need that home base, because I am so very changeable myself. I need that structure. I need the anchoring. I need the boundaries. I need the safe place where the chaos of me could find its place and bounce around without fear of loss or damage.

But the further I traveled on that road, the more I understood that a rubber room only works for so long. Religious practice should not be a way to escape from the world. I will always be looking past Loretta Avenue toward the busy streets beyond—to Overlook and Coronado and Glenway avenues.

I will outgrow the curfew and the safe container, because the world is loud and bright and wonderful. I will want to be a part of it, and that is right and true.

The practices of prayer and fasting, liturgy, mystery, and community are not intended to build places for me to hide. They are designed to anchor me to something deeper, something lasting, something I take with me when I cross the street, looking both ways, stepping out into the great, wide world. I don't really need a rubber room, but it might be nice, for a while anyway.

CHAPTER 26

DIVINE MYSTERY

(on entering in)

*To whatever church you come, observe its custom, if you
do not want to suffer or give offense.*

—St. Ambrose of Milan

*I resign. I wouldn't want to belong to any club that would
have me as a member.*

—Groucho Marx

Every week for a year, one of my boys would ask if I was
going to get in line for communion, and every time I
would tell them I could not take communion yet because
I was not yet chrismated. Communion was a members-only
event, closed to anyone outside the faith. When the practice

began, after Jesus blew town, the meetings were secret; the followers were careful. Catechumens were only allowed to witness the first part of the service. Even now, in some places, the Liturgy keeps the line "Depart, ye catechumens" in place, not strictly as an instruction but rather as a reminder that we're moving into another moment, another holy place. In past times, perhaps the catechumens would leave to get more instruction on the faith, or maybe they just moved blinking into the afternoon sun, wandering a bit, mulling it all over.

Monica Coors was the one who told me we couldn't be friends freshman year. Most of my friends were in different classes. I didn't even share a lunch period with the girls I knew from St. Teresa of Avila, at least the girls I knew who liked me. I sat next to Monica and her friend Jenny at lunch, because I was assigned seats near them in all the classes we were in together. It seemed like a natural transition, and so I sat next to them at the lunch table while they talked about clothes and music. I knew nothing of clothes and music, but I listened and tried to learn. When I would chime in with a suggestion or an observation, they would pause, look at me, and then go on.

Social cues were never my strong suit. It seems I suffered from a sort of social cue dyslexia, missing some pieces, shifting others. That they would leave no room for me to sit after a few weeks did not register. I just found my way in, sitting where I could. While they made plans among themselves to see INXS, I listened, and when they wondered how they'd get to the show, I offered to have my mom drive.

In my own defense, the shape of Monica's mouth coupled with her thick braces meant that it was hard for me to tell when she was sneering. She always appeared to be sneering in my estimation. She passed me a note in the last class of the day, telling me we were not friends and asking me to stop sitting with them at lunch. For most of the school year, I sat at different tables, usually alone, always searching for some sign of acceptance and welcome. Belonging was a struggle.

Thank God, my boys no longer feel compelled to refer to communion as "snack." For the first few years of church attendance, no matter how many times I explained it to them, they continued to view it as simply a break in the monotony. Snack time. When we attended the Anglican church in Nashville, they were gutted to realize they were not eligible to receive "snack" because they were not baptized. They begged to be baptized, because they wanted to be a part of the lineup for the bread and wine. At that time, Dave and I weren't sure what baptism meant to us or what it ought to mean to the children. We put it off, waiting for the right time, the right mindset, the right community of faith. But those things never lined up, so the children never moved toward the water and oil of baptism.

They were satisfied for a long time at the Presbyterian church we attended after that, with cookies every week in the foyer and communion snack once a month in the sanctuary. All were welcome, regardless of baptismal status, and we'd catch brunch out somewhere before the hour-long drive back to our house in the middle of nowhere. Food for the journey.

Forming the church plant we called Metanoia meant we could make our own rules for the liturgy, for the community, for the taking of communion. All were welcome at our table so long as they were "clear" with the other members. The first rule of communion at the startup church was the rule of repentance, metanoia. If you had an issue with another person in the room, it had to be cleared with them; otherwise, abstain from partaking. Communion was about community, about relationship with God and with one another. All were welcome at the table so long as we were in right relationship with one another.

We took to that first communion together with gusto, and we moved off into corners to "clear" when it felt necessary. It took a long time, and then we broke the bread and took the cup to give thanks. When we approached for communion, we were asked what we "brought to the table." For some it was sadness or pain, and for others it was gratitude and joy. The one who offered the bread and wine would say, "Because of Christ's body and blood, you can have joy," or "you can have peace," or "you are forgiven." Each offering to the table was given an offering in return.

Communion was food for the journey, shared confession, shared celebration. It was intimate and revealing, beautiful and dangerous. We thought it was cutting edge, and we thought it was ancient. What we hoped we'd created to be inclusive, though, was, by its design, also unintentionally exclusive. We had designed a religious emotional nudist colony. When we had visitors to our small community, it was like asking them to take off all their protective clothing and then show us themselves, one piece at a time. The intimate community functioned beautifully for as long as we were all willing to get naked, but it assumed that anyone coming in would want to bear witness to that.

It was church and it was therapy, and for a long time it was all that kept our small family of believers alive in the culture of McDonald's and megachurches. We entered damaged, and when we began to heal and grow, when our Metanoia rehab was over, our numbers shrank as we peeled off one or two at a time to re-enter the world. When Metanoia closed its doors, the transition was complete, and we agreed that the place had done what it was meant to do. We learned what we were meant to learn, healed what we were meant to heal, and then we fanned back into the larger world of mainstream religion and 99-cent Happy Meals.

THE HOLY EUCHARIST IS FOR ORTHODOX Christians alone who have prepared themselves with prayer, fasting, and confession.

The Orthodox Church was the first place my infant baptism as a Catholic did not automatically grant me an entry card to a communion line, and I struggled with that. The Catholic Church kept an open offer of communion to Orthodox Christians, but the line did not work the other way. Orthodox understand communion as a sacred event, offered only to those people who enter into that community of faith wholly and freely, with nothing held back. It is an intimate act, sharing the cup with conditions agreed upon beforehand—baptism, chrismation, fasting, prayer, and confession.

From the outside of the practice, I watched as people lined up to receive, crossing arm over arm over heart—a humble position, a place of preparation. The choir's tune held the procession, surrounding it with song—Receive the Body of Christ, taste the fountain of immortality—and I watched and listened, thinking about that fountain and about being on the sidelines. I wanted to know what these people knew; I wanted to taste what they tasted and feel what they felt. It was the mystery that drew me in, the promise of healing, the promise of this one certain thing connecting us no matter what our history, our ethnicity, or our political leanings.

My third year as a catechumen, on Holy Saturday, I sat in the pew at Old St. Pat's in Chicago late in the evening. My friend and fellow writer Karen was being received into the Catholic faith. Her struggle to become Catholic was a mirror of my own becoming Orthodox in many ways, and we lamented the road blocks and stop signs and strange looks we got when we told people about the paths we'd chosen. Being a "cradle" Catholic, I could not offer a whole lot of insight to Karen. It's different to be born into a tradition. I took a great deal for granted. Karen was contemplative and intentional in her choosing to become Catholic. While I loved my time as a Catholic, ultimately it was always going to be my hometown, a place I loved but didn't want to live.

Karen made her way toward the pew before the Vigil began.

We talked about this next big step and about how nervous she felt, and just before she walked to take her place with the other catechumens, she offered that probably I could accept communion, since I was Catholic and since the Orthodox are welcome at the table there. But at that moment, I was not a practicing Catholic, nor was I yet Orthodox, and I thought about this for the length of the Mass. I was still in the muddy middle of it all, struggling still, always nearly there. Seeing this feast laid out before me, I was tempted to chuck it all and just go back to my hometown. I watched as people filed out one by one to join the lineup, the ushers coming to the end of each row to indicate that it was time. I wrestled those feelings of loneliness and impatience and jealousy, too, while I sat there, letting people file out around me to join in the feast.

A year earlier I'd had the same struggle sitting at a women's retreat I helped to lead. A few days before the retreat, I was asked to offer the bread and wine at communion. I mulled over the request. It was something I had always been quick to take into hand, a practice I'd developed and shaped; and yet I could not find the desire to lead this time, so I declined it with no real explanation. As I sat waiting and watching the familiar ritual unfold—the reading of the words, the invitation to come and partake, the instruction that all are welcome—I felt myself apart from the group: not judging, not condemning, just apart. Communion did not mean this to me any longer. It was something else, something specific, something ancient and new all at once.

I'd confided my struggle about whether or not to participate to a friend at the retreat itself. Her first advice was to enter in and take part, but after hearing my struggle with it, her next advice was to wait and pray, to see how it felt in the moment and go from there. I closed my eyes during the wait and did as she suggested. I prayed, struggled, swore a little, and sighed as inaudibly as possible until the final participants made their way to the table.

When the place was still again, the woman leading communion said, "Is there anyone else?" I pressed my hands together quietly in my lap, palm to palm, fingertips meeting, and I felt the flesh on flesh, rooting me to that moment. The retreat leader looked to me as I stood to move on to the offering of the benediction to close us and send us out into the wide world. I was only nearly Orthodox, no longer Catholic, never a Protestant, living in the muddy middle, walking toward the Mystery.

CHAPTER 27

WANT AND NEED

(on motivation and forward motion)

*Peace is truly the complete and undisturbed possession of
what is desired.*

—St. Maximos the Confessor

You can't always get what you want.

—The Rolling Stones

My grandfather was the "as seen on TV" king. He
loved to buy things from ads on television, especially late-night products. After he died, we went
through the basement discovering all kinds of treasures. We ran
across the "pocket fisherman" and the stackable cup system and
the handheld buttoneer, all immaculate, all still in their original

packaging. My mother and I take after my grandfather in this. I have a collection of things I have purchased on a whim or because I thought they were a good deal. Some of these things are unopened; some were opened and then never used. As I think back on the reason for this, I come to one conclusion—it wasn't what I thought it would be.

Someone commented to me once that he considered his choice to become Orthodox very carefully, because in his words, "It cannot be undone." Is it like a tattoo? Will Orthodoxy be written in my flesh once the chrism touches my forehead, my hands, and my feet? Will I be marked somehow? Will a falling away mean more to the fate of my immortal soul? What if it isn't what I want? What if it isn't what I need?

I'm afraid I will become Orthodox and it will not be what I want at all. I'm afraid I will enter in, take it on, drink deep, and the water won't be as sweet as I'd hoped. I'm afraid the water I have pined for will make me want to throw up, make me want to run screaming into a bottle of scotch and never come out.

The further I go in my conversion, the more afraid I become. I'm most afraid of making a mistake. What if, after years of changing my diet and my prayer life, dragging my children to Liturgy week after week, talking and grousing and ripping my sense of self to pieces, what if after all that I become Orthodox and I hate it? Worse yet, what if I become Orthodox and I never take it out of the box? Perhaps I will place my conversion on the home altar where I pass it every day and go on with my life, like buying a treadmill and then only using it to hang damp clothes.

The conversion becomes my pocket fisherman, something that sounded good at 11 PM and came with three easy payments of $19.95—only I had forgotten I never cared for fish. What if it isn't what I thought it would be?

I often thank God I did not have the nerve to follow through on those tattoo ideas I'd sketched into the angst-ridden journals I kept in high school. Sketches of my future tattoo littered the margins, changing every few months along with favorite bands and best friends. I thought little about the future of my aging skin, little about the looks I might get as a grandmother with an outlandish tribute to Jello Biafra or David Bowie on my bicep. I thought only of how cool it would be to make my body a canvas, to wear my outrage, my rebellion, to make myself art.

The constant was the want and the need. I wanted to stand out. I needed to be patient. I have a needle phobia, that played a part, but the design was the thing. I knew that whatever I had imprinted on my body was going to be with me until we parted ways. I would ask myself with each design, "Can I live with this forever?" Laser tattoo removal has come a long way since then, so forever might be negotiable. Still, I wanted to get a tattoo that I would want to keep forever, one that I wouldn't glimpse in the mirror and cringe, remembering the romantic notion that led me to the tattoo table in the first place.

It's not too late to quit, to turn around and never look back. I know that voice in my head. It is the cynical voice speaking its sweet saccharine sticky sounds in my ear, smacking its lips at the end of each phrase. No matter how quickly I turn my head, I cannot catch it, I cannot stop the flood of fears. And then comes the responsorial phrase—the driving need, the headstrong kid who doesn't think she needs anyone all that much, the permanent resident of the garden apartment chimes in—What if? What if?

WHEN THE GREAT SNOWSTORM OF '78 HIT Cincinnati, Ohio, I was 11. While school was called off, I was charged with the task of continuing to take orders for Girl Scout cookies. I had a deadline, and I had a goal. So much of my identity was wrapped up in Girl Scouts. Life at home was troubled and turbulent. It was loud, and I was lost. I wanted to be special. I wanted to be seen. Attending Catholic schools meant everyone I knew was Catholic. No one was special. But my Girl Scout sash was loaded up with reminders of who I was—fire starter, seamstress, poet, cook. It was important. I was important.

For an introverted and awkward kid, selling anything door to door was a stretch. But I was committed, I wanted that badge, I wanted that goal met, and so I dragged my younger sister with me through the storm, through the mounting snowfall, because I didn't want to go alone. It was the middle of the day, and everyone was home. Where else would they be in a city brought to a standstill by the great blizzard? Each neighbor commented on my activity, some chiding me for being out in the storm, some praising me for my steadfast devotion to overpriced baked goods. My sister was cold, and she complained as we slogged through the snow, now piled up, now freezing, our legs lifting higher and higher, house after house, to plow through, to keep from slipping.

"Keep going, don't stop," I shouted into the driving snow as I pressed on to the Harrigans' house. She was cold, but I kept going because I knew we were nearly there. I enticed her with baseless promises of hot cocoa and mini marshmallows, knowing full well I could not make good on the offer. I told her I would run her a warm bath and we would snuggle into the fort we had pieced together between our twin beds that morning of the first snow day. Keep going. Don't stop, because if we stop we'll be colder, because if we stop I will fail, because if we stop we may not beat this storm, we may be buried in the fear and the doubt and pain, and only this small promise of warmth is enough to get us through what seems like an impossible task.

What if after all this work I find I do not want what I have earned? What if it's not what I had hoped? Then I was struck by a blast of wind and the abject fear that after all this, I would still feel just as empty as ever. What if, what if, what if . . . and I turned to look at my sister shivering in the snow and at the soggy order form in my hand. It's enough. We're enough. "Let's go home," I said, walking back to where she stood crying in the cold and the damp. "We have what we want," I said. "We have what we need."

MAY THE COMMUNION OF THY HOLY Mysteries be neither to my judgment nor to my condemnation, O Lord, but to the healing of soul and body. For years as a catechumen, though I was not able to take communion at the Orthodox Church because I was not chrismated, I would say the communion prayers aloud with everyone else. I'd clutch my prayer book to shore up the soggy memory I blamed on parenting and middle age, and I'd recite the words along with the entire congregation.

Some of the people here had been saying these words their entire lives. They seemed to rattle them off as easily as I could still rattle off the prayer my dad would say before dinner on the nights when he was home. "Bless us, O Lord, with these Thy gifts which we are about to receive from Thy bounty, through Christ our Lord. Amen." I had given up that dinner prayer about blessings and gifts and bounties when I left home for college. After we had kids, we said the prayer Dave's family had used growing up. I let him lead that charge. I was just glad to have some kind of bounty on the table at all, I was so overwhelmed with parenting and transitioning.

Now at Liturgy each week, I would say the communion prayers with my fellow worshippers, and I would watch them move forward to accept the gifts. There was never a moment during which I did not want to get into that line. Though I did not receive, I sang along with the communion hymn, Receive the Body of Christ, taste the fountain of immortality, over and over, repeating the words, the simple rise and fall of the notes, the steady procession. It seemed strange that I would feel so motivated by a lineup to a mouthful of bread mixed with wine, but to receive would mean I was finally accepted, finally a full member.

Being able to stand in that line and receive that offering hooked me with acceptance and entrance into the Orthodox club. That was the prize that reeled me in and kept me pressing my nose against the glass, waiting until it would finally be my turn.

Each week at Liturgy when I spoke the words of the communicant, it was as though they reached deeper and deeper into me. I showed up and I kept showing up, and I kept saying the words and watching, and I pressed forward into the journey week after week. It was like walking through that snowstorm with my sister, going house to house to get what I wanted— to reach the goal, get that badge, to make my way finally into Orthodoxy.

Until one week, around Pascha that third year as a catechumen, I came face to face with the weight I carried, the tension between want and need. I had hoped to be chrismated, welcomed into the family as a full participant, in time for Pascha. That was my goal. But the timing was wrong, the schedules didn't work out, and I realized a few weeks into Lent that I would have to wait again. I swam through the disappointment, wanting this part of the journey to be over already. Tired of being a catechumen, tired of pressing my nose against the glass, at the same time I worried I might live to regret making the jump. What if it isn't what I want? What if it isn't what I need? What if?

The following week during communion, I listened to the prayers of the communicant instead of reciting them. I listened to the sound of the communion hymn as I stood with my back against the cold stone wall. I leaned my head back and looked up to the ceiling and wondered if maybe I should just give in to the voice in my head that told me to bolt, to find something easier. It's not too late to quit, to turn around and never look back.

The sunlight was streaming in from the top windows of the church. It was going to be a beautiful day; though the spring was colder than usual, the day was clear. Receive the Body of Christ . . . I followed the shaft of light down, the remains of the smoke from the incense and the candles congregating there in the column of light, dust motes dancing, floating, filling everything. Taste the fountain of immortality . . . I listened to the singing of the choir, the familiar rise and fall, the wide harmonies and the predictable nature of the notes, dancing, floating, filling everything.

A church friend approached me then, shaking me from that moment, handing me a piece of bread, the *antidoron*, meaning "instead of the gift." The antidoron was bread, blessed and broken, the raw materials of the Divine Mysteries, offered "instead of" the Mysteries. For a catechumen, it was as close as I could come. I was grateful for the offering of that bread at that moment, even as I felt it was not quite enough. There was something else I needed, even if I was not always sure it was what I wanted.

It occurred to me, watching the communion line move, watching each person in line place arm over arm across her heart, step forward to the cup, let the priest place the elements on her tongue, that this was a profoundly intimate act. To receive that mix of bread and wine, to believe it to be a divinely inhabited substance, to believe it could bring real healing, real redemption, real and lasting change, is an exercise in trust.

In that moment, I understood all those things and the tension of the now and not yet. I understood the pushing forward through the snow, my sister in tow. I understood the want of being accepted and loved, and I understood, too, the need to be healed. With the world pressing in from television and movies and computer screens, I wanted nourishment, but I needed healing. When confronting the pain from my past and the fears in my future, I wanted affirmation, but I needed healing. With family obligations pulling me apart, I wanted comfort but I needed healing.

Wanting to be loved, wanting to be nourished, wanting to be affirmed, and wanting to belong are not bad motivators, but it was never quite enough to get me where I needed to go. Belonging, affirmation, nourishment, and comfort are what I wanted when I put my feet on the road to becoming Orthodox. But the healing is ultimately what the Divine Mysteries offer, and the healing is what I needed. I may enter into Orthodoxy and find it is not what I want, but I will enter in still, in the hope that it is what I need.

CHAPTER 28

FEAST

(on being hungry and thirsty)

*I write entirely to find out what I'm thinking, what I'm
looking at, what I see and what it means. What I want
and what I fear.*

—Joan Didion

*There's a bit of magic in everything, and some loss to even
things out.*

—Lou Reed

The book presented to me was about theosis. As she
handed it to me, my godmother told me it was one
of her favorite books. The slim volume ran around
eighty-six pages. I flipped through it, having heard only a bit

about this Orthodox concept. She put her hand lightly on the book in my hand. "I read this all throughout the year. It's a lot to take in." She instructed me to read it slowly, savoring the words and rolling them around in my head and heart for a while before moving on. The first few pages were an easy read, and then the phone rang, or a kid needed a hand, or I was suddenly thirsty, because the world is like that—moving and fluid and loud.

Sometimes there are holes in the fabric of the chaos, and when I allow myself the time, I can put my fingers through and feel the warm skin underneath, as though, all this time, everything I thought was the flesh of my life turns out really to be just clothing. The way I dress up my life can be constricting and severe, garish and risqué, or soft and flowing like well-worn linen. When I allow myself the time, I can sit in that realization, knowing that so much of the busyness and stress is self-made. It's at that moment I do understand what I'm after in becoming Orthodox. I do understand, only briefly, that verse about the peace that surpasses all things. And then the phone rings, or a kid needs a hand, or I'm suddenly thirsty, because the world is like that—breaking in, being loud.

I knew I was supposed to take off my shoes so the priest could anoint the top of my feet with chrism, but I didn't know when. I knew I'd have to read a number of prayers and agree to some terms and conditions with a "yes" now and then, but I could not keep the details of the ceremony straight in my head. When I tried to write about it, to suss out the struggle and the anticipation, I found myself coming up empty.

I invited everyone. I had no idea what the etiquette for an adult chrismation ought to be, and by then I didn't care that much. I'd been walking the road for almost three years, kicking every shrub, turning over every rock, looking for signs and wonders, looking for improvements to my temper and attitude and diet, and finding myself lacking every single time. I considered quitting the pursuit of it, because it was countercultural and weird and old school, and the timing never seemed to work out the way I'd hoped.

I had to explain Orthodoxy to everyone who asked, and I was terrible at explaining it. When asked by friends and family why I kept it up, I could not explain it in a sentence or a paragraph or an essay. No matter how often I wrote about wanting to be in the club, I never could say at any given moment that I was ready. Though I tried to get other people to tell me when I was ready, it really was up to me to pull the trigger.

Being chrismated was a commitment. I took it seriously, and I did not want to do it wrong. I was eager and apprehensive at the same time. I felt a little crazy in that divide between my past and my future, waiting there, standing there, struggling there in the present moment, my hands outstretched, brushing both sides of the cold, damp walls of rock, my past on my left, my future on my right, East and West.

While unpacking a box after we moved to Chicago, I found my baptismal certificate. I was baptized about a month after I was born, at St. Rita's Catholic Church in Dayton, Ohio. It was just down the road from where my dad's parents had lived their whole married life. My mother lived there while my dad was away at war. I imagined her taking me and my older brother to St. Rita's on Sundays while he was away, week after week, watching us grow in a faith we'd been born into, in a church where they'd known my dad when he was as small as I was— before Chamanade High School, before the University of Dayton, before Korea, before Viet Nam. I imagined my mother, away from her own home and living with my dad's family, braving the trip to church every week with two small children, praying for my dad overseas, unsure of what the future would hold for any of them.

I tucked the baptismal certificate into *For the Life of the World* by Fr. Alexander Schmemann, one of the first books I'd read when I began to explore Orthodoxy and a book I'd only recently begun reading again. I noticed then that the certificate sat facing the page on which he wrote:

> *Centuries of secularism have failed to transform eating into something strictly utilitarian. Food is still treated with reverence. . . . To eat is still something more than to maintain bodily functions. People may not understand what that 'something more' is, but they nonetheless desire to celebrate it. They are still hungry and thirsty for sacramental life.*

My fingers brushed that dog-eared page as I read the words again and again. I was hungry and thirsty for the sacramental life. My hands felt the flesh of the life that lay under the fabric of chaos and clouds I'd built to resemble "real life," and I had a taste of it then—that peace, that certainty, that awareness of "something more"—and I knew I would never feel ready. No matter how long I practiced the Creed, I could not seem to stop stumbling over it. No matter how many books I read to understand the Liturgy or the canons or the sayings of the church fathers, I could not seem to fully take it in. No matter how many calendar alarms I set, I would always forget the fast or the morning prayer or the feast days. I was always lacking, always playing catch-up, and I never felt fully prepared.

WHEN I WAS IN MY FIRST YEAR OF MARRIAGE, my dad didn't call me at Christmas. It astounded Dave that I was not more surprised. No one had heard from him, and though my brothers tried to get in touch, all they got was silence. My dad had finally been diagnosed with PTSD and was told by his therapist that it might have been the worst case he'd seen in a while. My father's disorder was so ingrained, so long suffered, that it had woven itself into his life completely. It was nearly impossible to separate out who he was from who he ought to be.

Still, no one really knew what that meant in the grand scheme of things. He'd always been absent from us, so we didn't worry when he didn't call or show up at Christmas. I was more angry and disappointed than worried, and I sat down and wrote him a long letter, unraveling the years of disappointment, unraveling the years of built-up anger, unraveling the expectations I had always had for what kind of father I thought he should have been and should still be.

I released it all, and I told him that. I told him in the letter that I was letting go of all of it, and I told him that, going forward, I would simply be grateful for whatever level of relationship he was willing to offer. He was no longer obligated to try to act a certain way or call a certain number of times or say or do anything I thought a father ought to say and do. And then, after I baptized the letter with strong tears and some prayer, I mailed it and thought nothing more about it. It was as if an entire mountain was lifted from my back, and I was finally able to straighten up, to lift my head to the sky and open my arms wide.

A few months later, I was on a film shoot with Dave out of the country. We had a brief opportunity to check in at home and pick up messages. I had gotten a call from my dad's wife, telling me first, "I just want to let you know your dad is going to be okay," and then the details of his heart attack followed. She kept repeating through the details in the message that he was going to be okay.

I hung up the phone and relayed the information to Dave, who then wrapped his arms around me. I felt nothing. It bothered me that I felt nothing, and then it bothered me more that I imagined it would be something of a relief when my dad died and my historically unmet expectations for what a father should have been would be gone. It would be too late by then to hope for redemption, and I would move on. I fell into sobbing as I pondered this. I grieved that relief, and I grieved that disappointment, and I grieved that feeling that I was lacking and would always be lacking.

I still had not spoken to my dad or his wife when we got home from our trip. My mom and my brothers gave me updates. I felt numb and unconcerned, having left my grief for all I knew back in the hotel room in Guatemala. I sorted the stack of mail and listened to messages on the machine, and then I came across a large envelope from my dad. It had been sent while we were away, just before his heart attack. He had gotten my letter, and he had responded.

He began, "I am so sorry that I have hurt you," and a floodgate opened in me with those words. As much as I thought I'd buried the disappointment, adjusted my expectations, done the grown-up thing of acting mature and moving on and being the adult, I was suddenly six years old again, and I cried as that six-year-old for a long time before I read any more. I had been hurt, I was still hurt, and that wound was deep and persistent, tearing open again and again, an emotional stigmata that only drained me of the blood I needed to live. No matter how many times I tried to cover it up or sew the flesh together myself, I could not do it on my own.

My dad explained in the letter that he had not called at Christmas because he'd been clinically depressed. He did not offer it as an excuse but rather as context for what came next. He had become so depressed that he decided to leave town, to disappear from all of our lives finally and completely. He felt that somehow if he just left then, he'd be able to leave some space for us all to set things right in our lives.

He got into his car and began to drive south to Florida or

somewhere, anywhere. He took a few clothes, his journal, and two pictures, and he enclosed a copy of them for me to see. One was a picture of my siblings and myself when we were kids, in front of the Christmas tree, just before we headed out to Mass on Christmas Day. We were wearing our church clothes, and I was clutching a stuffed animal I'd gotten. I was smiling and happy and hopeful. The second picture was taken in Chicago around my wedding day. All four of us were again standing in a line, happy to be together, arms around each other. I was smiling and happy and hopeful.

Dad had only gotten a few miles out of Cincinnati when the highway patrol stopped him. A snowstorm in Kentucky was so bad they were closing the expressway. He had to turn back. Nature had conspired against him, and he felt God had sent him home. He said he understood that he'd disappointed me, and he said he was grateful for whatever relationship I was willing to offer him. He did not make promises to be a better father, because he knew he could not keep those promises. He only wanted to let me know that he'd heard me and that he was sorry.

My dad's letter and his heart attack did not fix us. It did not make us into completely new people without a history of injury and disappointment. There were still years after that during which my dad was absent and I was injured again. The letter and the heart attack were not enough, and could not be enough, to bring all the pieces of our family together; it was simply too late for that. But it did lift something new into us, from deep below the surface of the water. It lifted some hope, some redemption, some possibility, and it fuels us still. It carries us through the injury and the unmet expectations and the pain that comes with both. And it reminds us that we are human and we are loved, because while it is important for us to remember that we are all ash, it is more important to know we are redeemed. That makes us bold enough to keep reaching for love with long outstretched arms, heart open and willing and vulnerable.

IT WAS NEAR THE FEAST OF MY PATRON, St. Theodora of Vasta, and near my birthday. I was in Chicago in the fall, my favorite time to be in the city. I invited everyone, and I didn't care how it looked or what people thought. I made my confession, putting all my marbles on the table, and when the time came I kicked off my shoes, gave my "yes," closed my eyes, and accepted the water and chrism on my forehead, my lips, my throat, on my hands, my heart, and my feet.

It isn't like magic, or maybe it is a little like magic, if magic is the ability to suddenly see things new, see things we'd never noticed before. Maybe magic really is just revelation after all. I told my priest and later my godmother that I was realistic in my expectations of becoming Orthodox. While I'd placed a picture in my head of who I wanted to be, I had no real expectation that the application of oil and water mixed with prayer and commitment would transfigure me, body and soul, and that instead of cussing when I prayed I'd immediately be offered the visions and wonders of theosis. I had no goal in mind of walking from the church and being a different, more complete version of myself. I was trying to be realistic, trying to avoid disappointment. Presbytera smiled and shrugged a little. "Maybe you will," she offered.

My chrismation didn't fix me. It wasn't magic; it was conversion, if conversion is the ability to suddenly see things new. It lifted something to the surface. When the oil touched my skin, when it sank into my pores, it did draw out something ancient, something tucked away in me, primed and nurtured by the water, the reminder of my baptism, which took place before I could talk or reason or choose for myself. The touch of the chrism and the holy water on my forehead and my lips, my throat and my heart, my hands and my feet made manifest a vision of wholeness, made possible a path, made hope rise up from its long-hidden place under the water. If conversion really is revelation, it made me see my heart as open, willing, and vulnerable.

In some ways, though, I'll always be just nearly Orthodox, no matter how long I practice the Creed or how much I read to try to understand the Liturgy or the canons or the sayings of the church fathers. Becoming Orthodox was not about gaining a prize, something I could place on my mantel to show off at parties, and it was not about magic, making me suddenly into a new and improved version of myself. It was the first step on a long lifetime road, the conversion, from the Latin *conversio*, meaning "a turning around." This was the moment I turned to see where I'd been and where I was going next.

My chrismation didn't fix me, because I will always be in need of healing from the bleeding wounds I brought into the faith with me the day I was welcomed. I am always going to be healing, always practicing the faith, just nearly Orthodox—almost there, within reach, welcome at the feast, given food for the journey—because the road is long and winding, and it was never about the destination. It was always about the road.

About the Author

ANGELA DOLL CARLSON is a poet and essayist whose work has appeared in *Burnside Writer's Collective*, *Image* Journal's "Good Letters," *St. Katherine Review*, *Rock & Sling* Journal, *Ruminate* Magazine's blog, and *Art House America*. You can also find her writing online at Mrsmetaphor.com, Nearly-Orthodox.com, and DoxaSoma.com.

Angela and her husband, David, currently raise their four chaos-makers in the wilds of Chicago with some measurable success.

Recommended Reading

The Ascetic Lives of Mothers
A Prayer Book for Orthodox Moms
by Annalisa Boyd
Annalisa Boyd knows motherhood—its challenges, its joys, and its potential for spiritual growth. In this prayer book she offers a wide selection of prayers mothers can use to intercede for their families as well as to grow in virtue themselves.
• Paperback, 176 pages, ISBN 978-1-936270-95-8—$12.95*

The Scent of Holiness
Lessons from a Women's Monastery
by Constantina Palmer
Every monastery exudes the scent of holiness, but women's monasteries have their own special flavor. Join Constantina Palmer as she makes frequent pilgrimages to a women's monastery in Greece and absorbs the nuns' particular approach to their spiritual life. If you're a woman who's read of Mount Athos and longed to partake of its grace-filled atmosphere, this book is for you. Men will find it a fascinating read as well.
• Paperback, 288 pages, ISBN 978-1-936270-42-2—$18.95*

Children of My Heart
Finding Christ through Adoption
by Ashley Lackovich-Van Gorp
As a young professional working in Jerusalem, Ashley Lackovich-Van Gorp struggled to embrace her Orthodox faith with all her heart. She never dreamed her search for an intimate relationship with Christ would lead her to Ethiopia and into the hearts and lives of two little orphan girls—now orphans no longer.
• Paperback, 193 pages, ISBN 9978-1-936270-91-0—$17.95*

Following a Sacred Path
Raising Godly Children
by Elizabeth White
Practical advice for parents (and educators) on raising children to understand and love their faith. Includes activities the family can share that encourage children to discover spiritual truths for themselves and own them for life.
• Paperback, 144 pages, ISBN 978-1-936270-73-6—$13.95*